WITHDRAWN

RELIGIOUS IN THE 1983 CODE

RELIGIOUS IN THE 1983 CODE
New Approaches to the New Law

by Elizabeth McDonough, O.P., J.C.D.

FRANCISCAN HERALD PRESS
1434 WEST 51st STREET • CHICAGO, 60609

RELIGIOUS IN THE 1983 CODE: New Approaches to the New Law by Elizabeth McDonough, O.P., J.C.D. Copyright © 1985 by Franciscan Herald Press. All rights reserved.

Library of Congress Cataloging in Publication Data
McDonough, Elizabeth.
  Religious in the 1983 code.
  Includes indexes.
  1. Monasticism and religious orders (Canon Law)
2. Canon Law. I. Title.
LAW   262.9'4   84-18797
ISBN 0-8199-0884-3

Nihil Obstat:
  Rev. William Thomas Kessler
  Censor Librorum
Imprimi Potest:
  Sister Mary Ellen Lynch, O. P.
Imprimatur:
  James A. Griffin
  Bishop of Columbus
August 22, 1984

"The Nihil Obstat and the Imprimatur are official declarations that a book or pamphlet is free of doctrinal error. No implication is contained therein that those who have granted the Nihil Obstat and the Imprimatur agree with the contents, opinions, or statements expressed."

MADE IN THE UNITED STATES OF AMERICA

For all my Sisters

—with sincere thanks

Preface

This book is intended for the general information of religious who do not possess canonical expertise but who, since the recent promulgation of the new Code of Canon Law, may be interested in how the 1983 code affects religious life today. Most of its content has been presented in the form of lectures at workshops for religious concerning the new code in various cities of the East and Midwest in the United States during the past two years. The lectures have been committed to writing both as a response to queries about their availability from people at these workshops and in an attempt to meet the current need for general information about the new law for religious treated in a broad context and written in English.

Because matters affecting the people of God should begin (and end) with a consideration of the Word of God, Chapter 1 contains a brief summary of law for God's people in a former context—that of Paul's letters to the Romans and Galatians—and notes how the relationship between people and law may not have changed all that much in two thousand years. Because any perspective beginning only with consideration of contemporary circumstances is necessarily distorted (at best), Chapter 2 provides the reader with some background information on the transition from Paul's "you are free from the law" to the 2414 canons of the 1917 code and the 1752 canons of the current code. Because one of the main difficulties with church law is that people often do not understand its role and purpose, Chapter 3 explains the manner in which law generally functions within the ecclesial body and also mentions some of the limitations of this functioning.

Chapters 4 and 5 deal directly with the new law regarding religious. The former gives an overview taken from the canons of the 1983 code itself concerning the basic elements of religious life. The latter shows the basic organization of and changes contained in the 1983 code as well as the transitional norms—the law in addition to the 1917 code that has governed religious life in the two decades since Vatican II—that have affected the current code. Because some of this material is rather technical (not to say, occasionally tedious) more detailed information regarding this transition is contained in Appendices I–III with the hope that the less canonically oriented reader will not be tempted to omit this chapter and the more canonically oriented reader will not be disappointed. Appendix IV—also directed to the more canonically curious reader—provides a summary and interpretation of two recently issued transitional documents concerning the new law for religious.

The practical concerns of Chapter 6 have been chosen on the basis of those which tend to surface most frequently at lectures and workshops or are most frequently raised in canonical consultations with various communities. The three broad topics of this chapter also relate to many other aspects of the law concerning religious which are, whenever possible without being extraneous, included in the comments.

Chapter 7 has been included in the book for three reasons. First, the law regarding cloister for women is quite unique and generally not well-known. Second, an understanding of the history of cloister for women contributes immensely to a better understanding of apostolic women religious in the Church. And third, while little is written regarding this topic which is directed to and available for both cloistered contemplative and apostolic religious institutes, members of both types could benefit from more knowledge about the other.

Preface ix

The final chapter is an attempt to return again to the original context of the Word of God and to reinforce the importance of religious life as the following of Christ with all other matters—including law—ultimately and properly understood precisely and only in this context.

The reader should perhaps be cautioned that the entire book has been written to be accurate, balanced and readable. In this perspective, the chapters flow better and are more understandable when read as entire units and when read sequentially. An English translation of the canons on religious, a glossary of many canonical terms mentioned in the text, and a rather extensive index of both topics and canons cited are included simply to make the book easier to use as well as more informative. A bibliography or list of suggested reading has been deliberately omitted because (1) most of the material is contained in technical periodicals which would not generally be available to the reader and (2) the suggestions or citations would be rapidly outdated.

The contents of this book certainly do not exhaust the topic of religious in the 1983 code. Some matters, such as the property of an institute or dispensation from vows, are mentioned only in passing. Some canons—as can be seen in the Index of Canons—are not mentioned at all. Recall, however, that the purpose of this book is for general information of the canonically uninitiated reader. Nevertheless, the manner of presentation is definitely intended to be quite in keeping with the *aggiornamento* called for by John XXIII in convoking the council and announcing the revision, with the *novus habitus mentis* or "new way of thinking" urged by Paul VI in guiding the revision process, and with the "primacy of love, grace and charisms" in the Church mentioned by John Paul II in promulgating the new code.

Finally, a word of gratitude is in order for Amadeus McKevitt, O.S.U., who has been a capable and experienced copresenter in most of the above-mentioned workshops and whose thoughts have contributed to and helped in refining Chapters 2, 5, and 7. Similar thanks are due to Patricia Kozak, C.S.J., and Mary McCaffrey, O.P., who read the original manuscript and made suggestions for improving format, style and grammar, as well as to Ladislas Orsy, S.J., who made valuable suggestions for improving the theological and canonical content of the text.

Elizabeth McDonough, O.P.
The Catholic University of America
September 14, 1984

TABLE OF CONTENTS

PREFACE   vii

1 PAUL AND THE LAW   1
    The Mosaic Law and the Law of Christ   1
    The Internal Law of the Maximum   4
    Caveats for Contemporary Religious   5

2 EVOLUTION OF CHURCH LAW   9
    The *Ius Antiquum*   9
    The *Ius Novum*   12
    The *Ius Novissimum*   13
    The Pattern of Legal Evolution   16

3 THE ROLE OF CHURCH LAW   19
    The Purpose of Church Law   19
    Functions of Church Law   22
    Some Limitations of Church Law   24
    Minimizing Misuse of Law   30

4 ESSENTIALS OF RELIGIOUS LIFE IN THE CODE   33
    A Way of Life Following Christ   35
    Total Personal Consecration   36
    Public Vows   36
    Ecclesially Approved Institute   37
    Consequences of Approbation   37
    Summary of the Essentials   39

5 THE "OLD" AND "NEW" FACES OF THE NEW CODE	43
General Format	43
Specific Categories	44
The *Ius Vigens*	45
Major Changes	51
6 CURRENT PRACTICAL CONCERNS	57
Common Life	57
Obedience	61
Apostolate	68
Continuing Concerns	72
7 COMMENTS ON CLOISTER FOR WOMEN	75
Evolution of Cloister	75
From the Code to Vatican II	78
Current Legislation	81
A Deeper Look and Different Words	86
8 FURTHER CAUTIONS, SOME LEGAL FALLACIES, AND A FEW WOES	91
Further Cautions	91
Legal Fallacies	94
A Few Woes	97
APPENDIX I Chronology of the Revision Process	99
APPENDIX II Principles Guiding the Revision of the Code of Canon Law	101
APPENDIX III Additional Information on Interim Legislation	103

APPENDIX IV Transitional Documents	109
APPENDIX V Canons 573–709 of the 1983 Code	115
GLOSSARY	155
INDEX OF TOPICS	159
INDEX OF CANONS	163

Chapter 1
Paul and the Law

The Mosaic Law and the Law of Christ

The biblical notion of law is a very encompassing one. Since law for the Hebrews was considered as a pact or treaty made with God, it governed a relationship that could include every aspect of one's life. Moreover, in referring to law in the Old Testament, the term itself was not always used in a univocal manner. Sometimes "law" meant specific teachings based on a portion of scripture. At other times the word was used to refer to the first five books of the Old Testament known as the Pentateuch. Yet another use of the term was to refer to certain portions of the Pentateuch such as the commandments enumerated in Exodus 20.

When Paul uses the word law or **nomos**, particularly in his letters directed to the Romans and the Galatians, he is referring specifically to the Mosaic Law or that which is attributed in origin or in spirit to Moses. Paul says very clearly that this **nomos** is good and just and holy because it comes from God (Rom 7:12). He also says very clearly that this **nomos** has several important limitations: (1) it was a temporary thing, (2) it became an anomaly and (3) it has been replaced by the Law of Christ. The law was a temporary thing in that its role was much like that of a tutor or guardian who helps a child to learn or acts as a guide until the child is old enough to be personally responsible (Gal 3:24, 4:1–2). The law became an anomaly because this **nomos** that was good and just and holy was used by people in such a way that it produced evil effects (Rom 7:11–13). Finally, the former temporary Mosaic Law has been replaced by the Law of Christ which is the *new* **nomos** for all Christians (Gal 4:3–5).

It is important to note here that Paul does not say all law is abolished when he comments on freedom in the Spirit (Rom 7:6, 8:2). What Paul does say is abolished is the Mosaic Law or, more pointedly, the current understanding of that law in the minds and hearts of the Romans and Galatians of his time. There is for Paul—and for all Christians—a Law of Christ which obliges but does not coerce (Gal 6:2). There are certain actions—primarily dealing with how believers should deal with one another—to which all Christians are bound but which no Christians are in fact coerced to do (Rom 13, 1 Cor 5–8, Gal 5–6). What Paul actually does in regard to the obligations of the law is to reverse the principle of causality. The old law was external; the new law is internal (Rom 7:6). The "deeds of the law" performed from without are no longer efficacious; now only the "fruits of the Spirit" emanating from within are efficacious in the lives of the baptized (Rom 7:4). There is now only one important deed in all of reality, and that is the sacrifice of Christ Jesus to which all Christians are configured in baptism (Rom 6:3–8). Thus, for Paul, the new creation one becomes in baptism causes a death to living by the precepts of the law and enables a rebirth to living in grace with a powerful and dynamic law of the Spirit motivating from within.

The Mosaic Law was considered by the Hebrews as a means of justification before God, as something in and through which God manifested his word and will for the people, and as the sustainer of God's presence in the world (Ps 119). But the precepts of the Mosaic law became a tool of sin in the hands of those for whom it had become the ultimate reality. The Mosaic

Law did not foster life as intended but was distorted in such a way that people developed a mentality allowing them not to accept Christ and even to crucify him in their midst. Thus the entire law—along with its engendered legalism—is nailed to the cross with Christ. Paul uses a bit of rabbinical logic to say that Christ is both subject to all the precepts of the law by circumcision and "cursed" because that same law so refers to anyone who hangs on a tree. Thus Christ is able to carry all the curses of the law—which apply to anyone who does not perfectly keep every precept of it—to the cross and literally kills the legalism of the law which has led to his crucifixion (Gal 3:10–14). Christ is now the new law, the **telos nomou**—or goal towards which all strive in this great race of life (Romans 10:4). He has gone beyond all requirements of the Mosaic Law, which could not contain him, and has justified us all in the sight of his heavenly Father.

The justification accomplished in the crucifixion is no mere legal fiction, but is rather a transformation into the likeness of Christ for all those who in baptism are baptized "into his death" (Rom 6:3) and have "put on Christ" (Rom 13:14, Gal 3:27) as Paul says. Biblically, to be justified means to stand in right relationship with our Creator and God. The justification accomplished in Christ enables us to stand in right relationship with God because in baptism we are "clothed" with Christ. Thus, when we stand before God at final judgment, we stand *in* Christ who is *the* living right relationship with the Father. This justification has been publicly accomplished and is publicly attested to by the cross. Paul refers to the cross as a placard or road sign (Gal 3:1) displaying the incredible justice of God—that justice to which God has freely and irrevocably bound himself in his Word, who is Jesus. Note, however, that God is not bound to the Hebrews' or to the Romans' or to the Galatians' (or to our) *understanding* of his justice, but rather to the reality of this justice in itself. This incredible justice of God can perhaps be best described as his unswerving fidelity to be merciful (Gal 3:1). No matter what—and the crucifixion of Jesus is the clearest example of it—God will be faithful to his own infinite mercy toward us.

The Internal Law of the Maximum

The human counterpart of this incredible justice of God is the demanding freedom given to all Christians which can perhaps be best described as the internal law of the maximum (Gal 5:6). This internal law of the maximum demands that one always act in love (Rom 13:10), for this is the Law of Christ (Gal 6:2). This is the only law that is always authentic, always creative, and always binding: Christians are to act in love. It is also the only law that one can never totally fulfill, for sometimes we do not act when we should and sometimes we act but not in love. Christians bound by this law are free not because there are no norms in our lives but because there is an inner principle of vitality allowing us and helping us to accomplish what is expected to be done by believers. Apparent external observance of this internal law of the maximum does not capture its total meaning. Apparent external nonobservance of this internal law of the maximum does not necessarily mean there is an inner violation. The Mosaic Law could not contain Christ. So too, we—individually and collectively—cannot contain the Law of Christ.

In spite of his emphasis on internal motivation, Paul still adheres to the principle—which is both legally and philosophically sound—that one's external actions manifest internal realities. Usually for those who are truly dedicated and practicing believers the internal motivation of the Spirit is manifested in actions indicative of what one believes (Gal 5:22). A simple contemporary example of this principle is easily noted in the ecclesiastical legislation requiring reception of Communion at least once a year (c. 920). For those who regularly practice their faith, the law is seldom a concern because one's inner belief and motivation are regularly manifest in a manner far beyond the minimal requirements of the norm. For those who may seldom practice their faith but claim to be members in good standing of the believing community, the law is a reminder that what is claimed as an internal reality is not being manifested even in the most minimal manner, thus calling for a re-evaluation of the claim to actual possession of the inner motivation. Furthermore, Paul is quite clear in his opinion that we all need some law even though law—according to Paul—is primarily directed toward the unjust (1 Tim 1:8–9). Why do we need law? If we are basically honest, it can be generally asserted that we are all at least a little unjust. There are no spectators in the world of sin. Throughout history law appears to be a permanent part of organized society, with ecclesial society being no exception.

Caveats *for Contemporary Religious*

What, then, is the purpose of beginning an explanation of the new Code of Canon Law as it affects twentieth century religious with comments on the concept of law in Paul's letters to the Romans and Galatians? The purpose is twofold. First, if we believe that the Word of God is living and active, then Paul's approach to the Mosaic Law is not directed merely to his first century audiences but also—and perhaps very clearly at this point in time—to us. Second, if we believe that people act and respond within the same basic framework of humanity in any era, then perhaps we are no more or less prone to the errors and aberrations of interpretation and application with respect to law than were the Hebrews in the time of Jesus and Paul. In fact, we might well ask ourselves—individually and collectively—if the possible assumption of superiority by an isolated elite has not been (and cannot continue to be) a pitfall for religious as easily as it seemed to be for the Pharisees? We might well ask ourselves—individually and collectively—if our own brands of legalism do not create an ambience into which God-With-Us sometimes does not fit any more than Jesus fit into the well-patterned lives of the religious leaders of his day? We might well ask ourselves—individually and collectively—if the lure of theoretical perfection and abstract generalizations can become our operative principles protecting us from facing the tensions of daily reality?

Law—Mosaic Law or canon law or any other law for that matter—can be easily misused. Law in the Church is misused when it is allowed to assume an unwarranted autonomy disconnected from faith, theology and real life. Law in the Church is misused when it becomes a refuge for less than responsible people who desire no challenges from the gift of freedom. Law in the Church is misused when it serves as a panacea for the apparently well-adjusted, purely pragmatic people who merely cope with reality from day to day. Law in the Church is misused when it becomes an ultimate concern or becomes more significant than what is truly significant in the Christian dispensation. It is not so much the content of law as the exaggerated importance we can attach to it that is a problem. It was the same problem for the religious leaders of Jesus' time. Even though Jesus came as the perfect image of the Father, as the complete manifestation of God's will and as the fulfillment of the Mosaic Law lived in wisdom, a distorted approach to law enabled it to hold the Hebrews captive and to become a burden. This is precisely the accusation Jesus levels at the religious leaders of that time (Mat 23:3–4; Lk 11:46) and, perhaps, through the word of Scripture, is also directed to us here and now.

Law can also become a burden for Christians today and perhaps especially for members of religious institutes. If we learn some lessons from the past and respond to the promptings of the Spirit in the present, religious today can prevent law from becoming a mere means of establishing organizational controls for the smooth functioning of institutional bureaucracy. With knowledge and caution and intelligent application of the law, we may perhaps prevent the fostering of a legalistic mentality in which God-With-Us still does not fit and is recrucified here and now in one another by our own brands of legalism. It is helpful to recall whenever dealing with canon law that subtle distinctions, numerous precepts and encompassing prohibitions do not bring peace of heart or transform one into the likeness of Christ—only grace does that. It is important to recall that the Church is not primarily a political or legal reality however much it may appear so at times. It is important to recall that—as Paul says so well—peace and unity come only through the Spirit and not through the observance of any law which in itself has no power of itself. It is important to recall that the fundamental Christian commitment is an internal and moral one depending on relationships among persons—mirroring the relationship among the Persons of the Trinity—whose life within us should be manifest in our lives. Law should not oppose or stifle that inner life, but there is potential tension between the basic structure of the law and the basic creativity of the Spirit. Jesus did not escape that tension in lived reality: neither will we. The evolution of canon law is, in fact, the record of that tension in the lived reality of the history of the Church.

Chapter 2
Evolution of Church Law

The Ius Antiquum

Law in the Church has a long history that can be divided roughly into three major eras the first of which is known as the *ius antiquum*—or old law—spanning approximately the first eleven centuries. There is evidence of some loose organizational structure in the Church even in the first few hundred years, but the type of structure differs depending on which Scripture accounts one follows (the Acts of the Apostles or some of the Epistles). Yet it is quite evident that there was then no highly centralized organization and no canon law as we know it today in the Church. There were local "synods" or gatherings of the clergy and faithful of a particular worshipping group with their leader or bishop in order to solve local problems and make *ad hoc* decisions. These *ad hoc* decisions touched on both disciplinary and doctrinal matters since the two were often connected. A typical example of such decision making would be how to deal with believers who had fallen away from the faith (and were therefore called *lapsi* from the Latin to fall or slip) and who then wished to be re-admitted into the Christian community. Since different circumstances and different people were involved in these local decisions, the results of such synods were often dissimilar—even for comparable problems—and applied only to the local churches for which they were made. Whatever the decision, however—as is the case with most church legislation, the results manifested something about belief (i.e., was baptism efficacious once and for all regardless of later falling away?) and something about behavior (i.e., what actions were expected of those *lapsi* who were allowed to return?).

Very soon in the history of the Church there also appeared collections known as church "orders" or rule books and guidelines of how the Christian communities actually worshipped and were organized. Authorship of these church "orders" was often attributed to the apostles in an attempt to give these "orders" greater import among the people. Some of the best known "orders" are the *Didache*, or *Doctrine of the Twelve Apostles* (early second century), and the *Didascalia*, or *Teaching of the Apostles* (early third century).

Collections of the declarations of synods, sometimes along with collections of papal pronouncements and even of imperial legislation were evident by the third century. Often these were named after the locality to which they primarily pertained, such as the "Hispania" in Spain, or after the person to whom the collection was attributed, such as the "Isidoriana" for Isidore of Seville. Some of these collections were more inclusive than others and eventually became the nucleus for future canonical collections.

With the approbation of Christianity by Emperor Constantine in 313, the Church began to adopt an organizational structure much like that of the Roman Empire. It was shortly after this time that the territorial divisions of the Church became known as dioceses and provinces (terms used to designate territorial divisions of the Roman Empire), that the ceremonial garb of church leaders became similar to that of the emperor and his court, and that communication by decree and decretal letters began to be used extensively in the Christian community. With the fall of the Roman Empire a few centuries later in 476, the highly structured and empire-like church organization fell heir to numerous responsibilities left by the vacuum of power in Western civilization at the time. With the development of the Carolingian Empire around the year 800, church law was imported and imposed as civil law by Charlemagne who used one of the ancient collections sent to him by Pope Hadrian I.

Several important things might be noted about these centuries in the development of the *ius antiquum*. First, the Church and the world were divided into two key centers, one in Greek speaking Constantinople, the other in Latin speaking Rome—with other church centers being located for a while in Jerusalem, Antioch and Alexandria. Second, by the sixth century civil legislation (such as portions of the *Code* of Justinian, c. 534), writings of the church fathers (such as Basil and Jerome) and papal decretals were added to the collections of the "canons" (the Greek word for rule) from various councils and came to be numbered among the sources of church law for future ages. Third, the approbation of Christianity in the Roman Empire brought about the baptism of numerous but often less than enthusiastic Christians eventually necessitating attempts at much needed reforms in the seventh and eighth centuries. Some of these reforms—although rightly desiring to free control of church property and personnel from the power of civil leaders—used less than honest methods such as the creation of false papal decretals (known now as the pseudo-Isidorian Decretals) to assert and to centralize the power of the Roman church. Fourth, the imposition of church law as civil law by Charlemagne in order to help structure his empire led to the superficial embracing of Christianity by *de facto* nonbelievers, thus seriously weakening the foundations of faith in the broad based Christian community.

The Ius Novum

In the twelfth century two major events in canonical evolution occurred: (1) ancient Roman Law texts were discovered and began to be studied in the early medieval University of Bologna and (2) a Camaldolese monk named Gratian compiled all the then extant canon law into one large collection called the *Concordance of Discordant Canons* (or *Decretum* for short). The first provided the conceptual framework for centuries of future study of canon law which was soon to become a separate area of scientific investigation in medieval universities. The second provided the text containing the canonical sources for this study.

Gratian's *Concordance of Discordant Canons* was precisely that: an attempt to find and to make some coherent canonical sense of numerous *ad hoc* declarations contained in the various collections of synods, councils, writings of the Fathers and papal decrees. Gratian's monumental *Decretum* became the systematized source studied by and commented on by future canonists, including a series of canonist popes beginning with Alexander III in the second half of the twelfth century. The *Decretum* was not an official collection of canon law, but its documents and comments—whether from councils or popes or Gratian himself—grew in authority as it was used more and more as a key source for church law.

In 1234 Pope Gregory IX (1227–41) commissioned the Dominican Frair Raymond of Penafort to gather the first major official collection of canon law which consisted solely of the decretals of Gregory. Collections of decretals of later popes were added to this collection until, by the beginning of the sixteenth century, the *Decretals* comprised a volume as large as Gratian's *Decretum*. The *Decretals* were also studied and commented on by numerous canonists with sometimes lengthy notations and multiple cross references (called "glosses") being

Evolution of Church Law 13

written in the margins of the manuscripts themselves, and sometimes even collected in separate volumes. Soon the two great volumes, the *Decretum* and the *Decretals,* were combined into the *Corpus Iuris Canonici* or "body of canon law" which—along with the commentators—became the primary source of church law and canonical interpretation for several centuries.

In the era of the early Renaissance, canon law felt the effects of the breakdown of late medieval philosophy and theology. At the same time the Church and the world itself were experiencing major transitions due to new discoveries in exploration and trade, the development of more independent nations and conflicts of power, and the devastation of the Black Plague and almost constant warfare. In the aftermath of the Avignon papacy (1309–78) the Great Schism (1054), and the Western Schism (1378–1415) and with the final fall of Constantinople (1453), seeds of geniune discontent and widespread misunderstanding gave rise to the Reformation. The Church's response to the Reformation was the dialectical retrenching of the Council of Trent (1545–63). A major contribution of Trent to the canonical arena was mandating publication of a corrected "Roman" edition of the *Corpus Iuris Canonici* in 1582, with all translations, commentaries and "glosses" forbidden, thus effectively terminating any creative canonical development for three and one half centuries to come.

The Ius Novissimum

The first official codification of canon law was called for by the bishops at Vatican Council I in 1869–1870. The *Corpus Iuris Canonici* with its many medieval commentators and the number of papal pronouncements and other legislative decrees from the period since the Council of Trent had resulted in a mass of canonical material difficult to locate, often contradictory, and even more difficult to understand and to reconcile. Work was begun on the "code"—something the Church had never before had in the realm of law—in 1904. The completed *Codex Iuris Canonici* or "code of canon law," in contrast to the medieval *Corpus Iuris Canonici* or "body of canon law," was promulgated in 1917 on Pentecost Sunday, taking effect one year later. It was an organized, exclusive (i.e., abolishing all former contrary laws), official text codifying the turn-of-the-century image of the Church. It was a great simplification of the morass of previous canonical legislation and thus was a valuable contribution to the Church in the early twentieth century. Nevertheless, it did tend to solidify much of church structure and practice at a time when most of the world—as in the transition from the Middle Ages to the Renaissance—was experiencing major changes. Therefore, subsequent decades resulted in numerous questions, adaptations and interpretations of the 1917 code until, by the time of Vatican Council II, it was obvious that a fresh vision of the Church required at the same time a new look at canon law.

When Pope John XXIII convoked Vatican Council II on January 25, 1959, he simultaneously mandated the revision of the 1917 code. An official commission for revision of the code was named in 1963, but its members decided to delay the revision process until after the conclusion of the council. When the council terminated its work, the revision process continued under the encouragement, guidance and direction of Pope Paul VI. The commission soon prepared ten principles to be used in the revision process, and these principles were approved by the first Synod of Bishops in 1967. Included among these principles were the call to maintain a juridical text and yet to foster a pastoral approach to law, to incorporate all post-Vatican II legislation and to include the exercise of subsidiarity as envisioned by Vatican II, to enunciate the rights of persons in the

Church and to protect these rights with appropriate procedures, to retain the basically territorial structure of the Church and to provide a new systematic arrangement of the code based on the concepts of Vatican II.

The commission then assigned various portions of the code for revision by different study groups. Upon completion of their work, these groups circulated the revised versions—in the form of *schemata*—among bishops, episcopal conferences, ecclesiastical faculties and some major superiors for comments and further suggestions. Eventually a comprehensive draft of the proposed new code was completed in the spring of 1980 and distributed for final suggestions. The 1980 draft with suggested alterations was submitted as a completed text to Pope John Paul II in the fall of 1981. Subsequent promulgation of the revised code on January 25, 1983, taking effect on November 27 of the same year, is now well-known to the Catholic church community.

In general the product of the revision process is a welcome improvement to the former 1917 code. It is shorter (1752 canons instead of 2414 canons), basically follows the "teaching," "sanctifying" and "governing" functions of the Church as enunciated at Vatican II (instead of following the divisions of Roman law or other civil codes), and has simplified much legislation by incorporating what canonists refer to as the *ius vigens* (or actual practice of the law as it is at present). Although some have criticized the rather limited consultation for the revision process—it was sent to restricted persons or groups, the *schemata* were in Latin and some items received little or no response—it is important to note that the current code is the result of the most widespread input of any legislation in ecclesiastical history. However, more important than the process of revision—and in some ways even than the product—is that this new law be correctly understood and applied in its post-

Vatican II context. The purpose of law in the Church must be kept clearly in mind lest it be given inappropriate significance and even misused as can be any human instrument in society.

The Pattern of Legal Evolution

Throughout the development of law in the Church a certain sequence of events is evident, namely that of a crisis followed by legislation in response to the crisis followed by a period of stabilization eventually followed by another crisis. The pattern is noteworthy because from it one can gather that ecclesiastical law is often a dialectical response to particular, historically situated circumstances. Likewise, church law evolves only in the context of the real world in which this Body of Christ that we call the Church exists.

The evolution of law specifically for those known as "religious" in the Church is a good example of the phenomenon just described. The first few centuries saw the development of hermits and holy ascetics (Antony in Egypt, c. 270) and some attempts at common life (Pachomius, c. 325; Basil, c. 360; Augustine, c. 390) partly in response to the popularization and lessening of fervor in "official" Christianity. Benedictine monasticism originating in the early sixth century dominated the known Christian world for several hundred years and was part of Charlemagne's imposition of Roman ways on his empire. But the laxity engendered by such global imposition—along with other conflicts of control and possession—led to the reforms of Cluny (c. 910) and Citeaux (c. 1098).

In the early Middle Ages the historical circumstances of the Crusades gave birth to the "military orders," like the Hospitalers and the Templars. The rise of towns and universities in the high Middle Ages provided the newly founded "mendicant orders" an ambience to meet the challenge of their new notion of not-so-monastic religious life. The turmoil of the Reformation era provided the context for founding the Society of Jesus (c. 1540) and attempts to found similar societies for women, such as the Ursulines (c. 1535), the Visitandines (c. 1610) and the Daughters of Charity (c. 1633). However, because the ecclesiastical world—in keeping with the rest of the world at the time—saw little or no possibility of activity for women in the public sector, such groups for women were compelled either to adopt cloister or to exist apart from official church recognition as "religious." Ecclesiastical approbation at the universal level for such groups of women "religious" was delayed until the time of Pope Leo XIII in 1900.

In our own century a form of consecreated life known as the "secular institute"—in legal contrast to the "religious institute—has emerged. Currently ancient orders are adapting their structures, and more recent apostolic foundations of both men and women are adjusting their life and activity to the realities of the post-Vatican II, twentieth-century Church. All of these inspirations and alterations in response to various crises, to historical circumstances and to new ideas from the Spirit have required legal clarification at certain points of development. The result of this ongoing legal clarification is the body of universal and particular legislation referred to as "religious law." But before investigating this current body of religious law, let us look briefly at the purpose, function and basic limitations of law in the church as such.

Chapter 3
The Role of Church Law

The Purpose of Church Law

Of the many purposes for law in the Christian community three key ones are service, order and balance. Law properly used serves both the mysteries of theology and the People of God, provides order and stability in the worldwide, visible ecclesial community and helps to balance articulated and recognized values. The mysteries of theology are served by law when external, practical norms regulate the related circumstances of theological and sacramental realities but do not attempt to efficaciously define or to outwardly dominate the mysteries. An example here might be the initial canon of the new code in the section on the Eucharist (c. 897) which uses the language of the conciliar document on the liturgy to describe this sacrament—among other things—as that in which Christ is contained, offered and consumed and through which the whole Church lives and grows. Obviously, this canon, in attempting to describe the Eucharist by using theological terminology as a foundation for the norms to follow, does not make this sacrament be what it is. The grace of God does that. The well-stated theological prologue in c. 897 merely gives a proper context for the norms on celebration of, participation in and reservation of the Eucharist. The intelligent reader of the code recognizes theology as theology and mystery as mystery and both of these as distinct from legal norm.

The People of God are served by law through the application of the legal presumption that baptized adults are intelligent, free and responsible persons. This presumption is, of course, not always true. Adults. as well as children, have varying levels of intelligence and knowledge. No one is completely free in all matters all of the time. And there are times at which even the noblest among Christians would rather not have to be responsible. Yet the law presumes that we are intelligent, free and responsible as a clear sign in the Christian dispensation of the fundamental respect to be accorded each individual. It is far better to begin with this presumption as a legal foundation than with the contrary presumption in which persons would constantly have to prove themselves worthy of treatment as adults, which would be a great disservice to the People of God as such.

Law provides order and stability in the worldwide visible ecclesial community by commanding what is good, forbidding what is evil, permitting what is indifferent and coercing observance in certain limited situations. These four actions attributed to law stem from the philosophical understanding and definition of law underlying the code. But the basic definition of law which is fundamental to the understanding of church law in general is not contained in either the 1983 or 1917 code. It is taken from the *Summa Theologiae* of the medieval Dominican saint and doctor of the Church Thomas Aquinas, and it states that law is an ordinance of reason formulated by one who has care for the common good and promulgated. Thus the law does not command **everything** that is good or forbid **everything** that is evil, but only those things which are important enough to be done or important enough to be avoided for the sake of the social body. In this context one of the law's primary purposes is precisely to provide a certain order in and stability of behavior so that these reasonable actions can be put into practice by reasonable people for the general benefit of the community.

Note that it is not the purpose of law to provide innovation. Law usually lags somewhat behind current experience because it basically follows life and does not dictate or create reality. Thus, those who look to the law for a prophetic stance or for futuristic vision will always be disappointed and sometimes quite frustrated. Genuine prophets are those who regularly meet the *status quo* of contemporary Christianity in any age with the deeper challenges of the gospel message. This is not the role of law. If history can remind us of anything in this matter, however, we might do well to recall that the prophets of any age are usually stoned by their contemporary legalists. The purpose of law is neither to be prophetic nor condemning but rather to provide a sound basis or skeleton on which people can grow and from which real prophets can re-echo perennial Christian challenges.

Another purpose of church law is to help believers in balancing fundamental Christian values. It does this by contributing to the interplay of a threefold fidelity: to the legal norm, to the truth of factual situations and to the real life process of evolution. If norms are genuine laws within the notion of law as mentioned above—that is, if they are reasonable, properly formulated, for the sake of the common good and promulgated—then in themselves they have some value and are worthy of observance. But, since the law operates on various presumptions—such as the one previously mentioned about intelligence, freedom, and responsibility—and since presumptions can be contrary to the truth, the value in the dictates of the law must be balanced with the value of truth in particular circumstances. Likewise, since norms of law are rather static entities, whereas human beings are living, dynamic creatures and since existence moves and changes from moment to moment and day to day, the value of any legal norm must be balanced with the ongoing process of human growth and development.

Functions of Church Law

What exactly, then, does law actually do in the Church and how does it accomplish its purposes? Among other things it provides organizational structures, indicates fundamental interrelationships, guarantees basic rights and obligations, and requires certain useful procedures. The organizational structures of the diocese and parish with which most are familiar are prime examples of the "skeleton" or "backbone" provided by law for the worldwide, visible ecclesial community of the Church. For religious, similar examples are the structures of orders and congregations, unions and federations. Often we do not advert to the inner workings of these structures unless necessary which, in itself, is a rather good sign that the law regarding them is sound and functioning well. For, like a good and healthy skeleton, law should be there as the structural foundation. But if laws—like the bones of a skeleton—become a constant concern, this is a sure sign that something is wrong, either in the structure or the situation or the people involved.

Law has another very important function of indicating basic ecclesial interrelationships which are directly or indirectly sacramentally based. So, for example, one attains ecclesial "personhood" by the sacrament of baptism. One cannot become a member of the Catholic Church in the manner that one obtains a credit card or joins a club. Entrance to the Catholic Church is **sacramental**, but the sacramental action has **juridical** consequences—that is, it has results which have legal effects in the public arena of the Church. The juridical consequences of baptism result in numerous rights and obligations for believers. Similarly, the juridical consequences of matrimony result in numerous rights and obligations for spouses, and the juridical consequences of sacred orders result in numerous rights and obligations for clergy.

In addition, some relationships in the Church are indirectly sacramentally based, such as those rights and obligations which arise from choice or function. Those who have freely pronounced vows in an institute of consecrated life—a life fundamentally based on the sacraments of initiation—have certain rights and obligations that others do not have precisely because they, and not others, have made this choice. Likewise, within institutes of consecrated life certain persons have rights and obligations that arise from particular positions, such as those of major superior or treasurer. The great function of the law here is to delineate those instances in which one has the freedom and ability to act without the imposition of negative sanctions (i.e., a right) or in which one has the responsibility and perhaps even requirement to act in order not to incur negative sanctions (i.e., an obligation). Practically speaking, this is the function of law that helps one know just where "the buck" actually does (or is supposed to) stop—a rather valuable service it would seem in the human and business affairs of any institute, ecclesial, or otherwise.

Finally, a key function of church law is the delineation of useful procedures in such a way that rights are protected, transitions are made smoothly and general upheavals are avoided. Persons approaching an ecclesiastical tribunal are protected by nondispensable procedural laws which require all steps of the process to be uniformly applied and all participants in the process to be qualified and nonprejudicial. Members of a religious institute are aided, as well as protected, in the matter of elections by qualifications and methods being carefully delineated beforehand in the code and in the laws of their own institute. The election of someone as bishop of Rome (i.e., the pope), although having separate, rather elaborate and pageantry-filled norms, is another example of procedural law in the Church which is often not adverted to for many years but serves well when needed. Again, like the good skeleton, good law does its job in a quiet and unobtrusive but very substantial manner.

Some Limitations of Church Law

To look at the purpose and function of law in the Church and not at least briefly at its concomitant limitations would be a great disservice since its limitations are "legion" and some are of greater import than others. To name only a few, law is limited by operating presumptions, by different literary forms, by various levels of documentation, by the context of its formulation, by its external nature and especially by human misuse.

That law operates on presumptions has already been mentioned, and the presumptions of law are many: people are presumed to know the law; words are presumed to mean what they say; people are presumed to say what they mean, etc. Presumptions are used by all legal systems to provide for ongoing functioning without having to decide simple matters every time they arise (such as, what legal word has what defined meaning) or for maintaining general order (such as, not stopping for a "stop" sign results in a penalty even if you did not know the meaning of a "stop" sign or did not see it). The problem with presumptions is that they are often not true—truth here being understood as that which actually corresponds to reality—and this can be a serious limitation for otherwise fine laws. Obviously, not everyone knows the law. Previously, canon law was only available in Latin, not exactly a commonly known language today, and even among those who knew Latin and studied the law for years, one would be hard pressed to find someone bold enough to claim total knowledge.

Now that the code is available in various modern languages more people may be able to read what it says, but this in itself has a built-in danger of equating being able to "read" the law with being able to "know" what the law really says and means.

This brings us to the problem of the other presumptions mentioned, because laws are a form of communication written in words. The meaning of a word often changes with time, and even well-chosen words do not always convey what the writer means. So, for example (at least in the recent past), grass was something that grew on the lawn and pot was something used in cooking. Neither word has only those simple meanings today. In ecclesiastical terminology, the word "heretic" does not have the same meaning after Vatican II as it did before; neither does the word "clergy." When the meanings of words evolve, the presumptions of law sometimes lag behind this reality and can cause limitations in understanding. Likewise, people—even word-conscious legislators—often do not say exactly what they mean to say. It can be the case that what the legislator wishes to accomplish by a certain legal norm simply is not stated in such a way that the person carrying out the norm in good faith is acting in a manner that will accomplish what was intended. People with any degree of experience in religious life can usually provide typical stories of being told to do something, doing it, and then being told it was not what you were supposed to do—even though is was exactly what the person said (or, rather, thought he or she said) to do. The purpose here is not to point out the communicative foibles of those giving directives but to note that law, as a form of communication, is subject to this common limitation in communication.

Literary forms in law are another of its limitations, especially if the reader is unaware of their existence. For several decades literary forms have been recognized in Scripture and used as a distinct aid in reading and understanding the Word of God. Thus, one does not read the Psalms in the same manner as one reads the parables or in the same manner as one reads the Acts of the Apostles, because they are different types of literature written in different styles with different purposes. In recent years it has been helpful to apply the notion of literary forms to church law as well, enabling one to read an "exhortatory" canon differently from a "theological" canon and differently from a simple "norm of action" canon. As in Scripture, this approach to legal texts also helps in understanding the meaning being conveyed.

A common lack of legal knowledge can also lend multiple possibilities to the limitations created by various levels of documentation. Basically there are three elements at which a canonist looks to determine the legal import of any document: the type of document, its source, and its content. Since Vatican II the Apostolic See has issued nearly two dozen different types of documents. For pontifical documents some, such as an apostolic constitution or a *motu proprio,* are usually legislative; whereas others, such as an encyclical or circular letter, rarely introduce new laws. Other documents, such as norms and instructions, are binding directives for implementing laws contained elsewhere, as in canons or decrees. Generally speaking, the Congregations of the Roman Curia do not have legislative power as such and for the most part issue decrees for certain groups or responses to particular questions or publish directives and policies indicating how laws are to be implemented. The source of a legal document is also important because conciliar constitutions or decrees are in a different category than decrees of a diocese or of a particular episcopal conference. Furthermore, the content of any legal document must be carefully investigated because sometimes even generally nonlegislative documents—such as instructions—change previous laws when those who issue the document have a specific mandate to do so. The point, of course, is that the informed and intelligent reader of the law does not treat all documents in the same manner because the legislator does not intend them all to have the same legal import. With a little information and a little practice, intelligent and informed reading of documents can be both informative and rewarding, especially when one no longer has to depend on the often distorted public media versions of what someone in the Church supposedly has said.

Another limitation of law—and one that is difficult to discern in our own context while being rather obvious in the context of other eras—is that of the historical, philosophical, theological and cultural conditioning of the law. For a better idea of the extent of contextual influence, let us glance briefly at the historical phenomenon of the Inquisition. It represents an ecclesial reality and era when, in point of fact, duly authorized members of the Church went about vigorously killing bodies in order to save souls. Philosophically, it was rationalized that the soul was the "form" of the body and therefore ultimately more important than the "matter." So the "matter" was sent to the rack and the pyre while God in his wisdom and justice could certainly sort out the worthy and unworthy "form" concerned. The only problem was that the whole procedure was very hard on real people (body and soul). It was all done quite legally and—at least ostensibly—in the name of protecting fundamental truths and genuine faith, while different interpretations of the same truth and faith somewhat readily transformed good and learned former friends into mortal enemies.

A comparable problem of contextual conditioning existed regarding the question of marriage as studied during the Middle Ages. A theological debate surfaced at that time in history regarding what constituted the essence of marriage. Some theoretical medievalists insisted that consent (i.e., basically saying "I do") confected the sacrament, while other (perhaps the supposedly more "worldly" ones) held that subsequent marital intercourse certainly had something essential to do with marriage. The medieval construct used was basically searching for a timeless certitude that would be retroactive as well as henceforth valid. The marriage question was no idle one because, in this philosophical construct, any definition with legal consequences had to include the ecclesiastical first family (Mary and Joseph) as validly and legally married. The only problem was that this led to an historically, philosophically and theologically conditioned discussion of marriage that became quite reductionist, if not inadequate to lived reality, in its legal expression.

Let us note that, even in our own era, turn-of-the-century theology regarding the Church, laity and religious life highly conditioned the legal contents of the 1917 code. In it papal legates appear as superior to bishops and religious appear as superior to laity—clearly notions that have been totally reversed by the proclamations of Vatican Council II. The current problem is primarily one of perception. We who are immersed in our postconciliar context cannot see the contextual aberrations caused by our own times that have been incorporated into the 1983 code as easily as we recognize the medieval or turn-of-the-century ones just mentioned. That does not mean, however, that this limitation of law is not actually there for us today.

Finally, if any limitation of law is all-encompassing, it is that of general human misuse. In fact, all of the above limitations could be subsumed into this general category because the law as a human instrument implemented by humans in human situations is inevitably subject to the plethora of human foibles. Perhaps we owe it to ourselves to take ourselves and our limited humanity in a more realistic and humble manner realizing that we are bound by what and who we are. The fault of much of the poor public image law sustains is not in the law—nor in the proverbial stars—but in ourselves. Human misuse of law generally falls into three categories:

interpreting favorably one's own cause, imposing legalisms, fostering antinomianism (or anarchy).

Interpretation is a phenomenon that occurs whenever anyone encounters and applies a law. There are strict rules in the code itself for how laws are to be interpreted. Most of us are probably aware of instances in which the same individuals apply the law differently in various times and circumstances. When we are the ones applying the law, it is usually easy to apply the same legal norm favorably for ourselves and our friends and perhaps less favorably for others. The law itself does not allow people to be judges in their own cases, and all day-to-day practical interpreters of law might do well to insist on the same operative norm for the sake of justice and equity in dealing with people. Legalism, or law for the sake of law and at all costs and in answer to all questions and problems, is a well-known phenomenon which has been the bane of ecclesiastics through the ages. There seems to be a certain penchant in the more religious type of personality that allows minutiae to be inextricably entwined with eternal salvation. Couple that with the general human tendency—admitted or not admitted—that most of us like to have most things our way most of the time, and throw in the structures and practices of centuries of religious life, and you have all the necessary ingredients for genuine legalism. On the other hand the opposite of legalism is antinomianism, or the intent or desire (or both) to do away with and to do without law. This approach seems more prevalent in our postconciliar days because there are some vague notions that we have been without law for all these years and, therefore, certainly do not need it now. Both are incorrect. The Church, and especially religious life, has not been without law all these intervening years since Vatican II, as subsequent comments on interim legislation will show; and history can attest that not many people do well for very long in the chaos engendered by an ambience of no law at all.

Minimizing Misuse of Law

Although the above suggestions of the numerous limitations of law may seem disheartening, there are ways to minimize its possible misuse:

> *First,* when in doubt, try not to absolutize. Doubt is lack of certitude and there is a human tendency when in doubt to settle uncertainties with personal *fiat* ("let it be," because I said so). Such arbitrary decision making often violates the truth and boxes people into even more unmanageable situations.
>
> *Second,* when in a "limit" situation, use a calm approach. A "limit" situation is one in which something must be done and the usual modes of procedure have collapsed. Often problems will unravel themselves by leaving well enough alone, and often the procedures presently in place can help us deal with the matter at hand. But sometimes nothing available seems to work and something still must be done; this is a genuine "limit" situation. In such circumstances it is characteristic of wisdom not to do anything desperate. By acting cautiously, one may not only be able to solve the problem more expeditiously but may also be considered somewhat wise.
>
> *Third,* do not let the judgment of those in authority prejudice what is the truth, even—or especially—if you are the one in authority. In fact all of us at some time or another exercise some type of authority over others. There is a tendency at such times to regulate reality more in conformity with our perceptions and desires than in conformity with the truth which actually corresponds to reality. Short of the exercise of the power of infallibility within the teaching magisterium of the Church in particular instances, the right to make a decision does not in

any way necessarily assure that one will make a correct decision or that one has a special corner on the truth.

Fourth, in limit situations always seek the facts, or—as the canonists say—be concerned not with *culpa* (blame) or with *poena* (punishment) but purely with *res facta* (the facts). Do not be satisfied in such matters with less than all the facts you can uncover pertaining to a particular situation and always be wary of the one who is only interested in the other side of the story if the other side is his or her own version alone.

Fifth, seek additional help whenever it appears a matter is exceeding your competence. Such help is not primarily or necessarily canonical, for there are many more effective ways to improve situations than by turning to the law.

Sixth, and finally, do not look to the law to solve problems in the first place, because solving problems is not a purpose or function of law. Law is very limited in "limit" situations and is merely able to indicate fundamental rights and obligations that must be respected and to require procedures from which one may not dispense.

In summary, there are many ways in the Church and in religious communities to accomplish our stated and desired objectives. Only one of these ways is law. Among others are education, communication and celebration. Law, although important and necessary, should not be looked to as a first means to accomplish what possibly can be done by other equally efficacious means. Law is enacted to deal with ordinary circumstances in the general course of human events and is not intended to provide legal options for every case that may arise in an articulation of the written norm. Law is a limited but useful human instrument that can be easily misused. Let us recall Paul's clear *caveat* to the Romans and Galatians that law in and of itself has no power whatsoever and that if we attribute to it more than it deserves we are rendering ourselves, one another and the Lord a great disservice.

Chapter 4
Essentials of Religious Life in the Code

The title of this chapter contains several presumptions to which the reader deserves a brief introduction before venturing further. The first is that the content matter herein is primarily life, not law. The second is that there is something about this life that is clearly identifiable, not merely nebulous and amorphous. The third is that some of the aspects of this life are substantive or essentials, that without which this life would not be quite what it is. And the fourth is that we are looking to the law to tell us something about the essentials of this identifiable life.

In addition to these presumptions, there is an operative principle being used here which is based on an understanding of the new code as an outgrowth of Vatican II and, like the Council, as something with both conceptual content and an ongoing impact. Practically speaking, we are looking at a legal reality base for religious life. Meanwhile, religious life has not yet plumbed the depths or foreseen the final implications of the transitions that have taken place in the Church since Vatican Council II. In this chapter we look to the revised code not so much for information as for some clear perspective, even from the code's legislative point of view, regarding substantive material about religious life which in itself is still evolving.

Finally, a minimal explanation of terminology is necessary so that the reader is aware that the canonical term "universal law" refers to that which is law properly speaking and which originates at the level of the Apostolic See—such as that which is contained in the 1983 code—and may be directed either to the entire Church or to a group within the entire Church, such as to the laity or to clergy or to religious. "Proper law" canonically speaking refers to that which pertains to a particular institute in the Church, such as law approved by a general chapter for the members of that religious community. The proper law of a religious institute includes the constitutions and other norms collected in various documents, by whatever name they are called, which indicate the rights, obligations, policies and operative principles of that institute. Although we are looking at the moment into the universal law contained in the 1983 code, namely cc. 573–606 on consecrated life in general and cc. 607–709 on religious institutes in particular, there are other universal laws that pertain to religious institutes. Furthermore, the proper law of religious institutes is required by universal law itself to specify matters in over one third of the canons concerned.

If these presumptions and operative principle are granted with the terminology as explained above being understood, and if repeated in-depth examination of the 1983 code with them in mind is conducted, the following can be seen as the substantive content of religious life as reflected in this code:

> Religious life is a way of life that consists in following Christ with consecration of the whole person by means of public vows in an ecclesially approved institute which results in certain structures and a definite incorporation into the local and universal church.

A Way of Life Following Christ

In the new code religious life is only one of many forms of consecrated life that consist in the following of Christ more closely (c. 573). In particular for religious, this following of Christ as proposed in the Gospels and expressed in the proper law of the institute is to be the supreme rule of life (c. 662), and in the religious community God should be sought and loved above all else (c. 619). It is the understanding of the code that in all institutes of consecrated life profession of the evangelical counsels of chastity, poverty, and obedience should be motivated by the underlying desire for an undivided heart (c. 599), for imitation of the self-emptying of Christ (c. 600) and for transformation into the likeness of Christ in the doing of his Father's will (c. 601). Consequently, all members of such institutes are obliged to fulfill faithfully these counsels and to adjust or order their lives in accord with the obligations freely embraced as expressed in the proper law of the institute (c. 598). This is clearly in keeping with the previously mentioned notion that Christian adults are capable of making intelligent and free choices for which they are then responsible.

Note that the code's understanding of this way of life is not a compartmentalized one: this is for God, that is for the community, something else is for the apostolate and something else again is for me or my interests. The following of Christ envisioned here is precisely that—the following of Christ, not following any group or any apostolate or the letter of any law or even following our own understanding of what might be the spirit of the law. It is a following that cannot be done relying on one's own power; and, therefore, the code presumes on the part of religious a life of personal prayer, liturgical prayer (including the Eucharist and the Liturgy of the Hours), regular retreat, continual reconciliation, various sound devotions (c. 663) and ongoing formation throughout life (c. 661).

Total Personal Consecration

The following of Christ as religious is expressed in the code as a consecration of the whole person in a total gift by which one's whole existence may become continuous worship of God in charity (c. 607). Since this is the ideal, legal requirements for admission to a religious institute include assessment of the whole person regarding age, health, disposition and maturity in keeping with future expectations (c. 642). Formation looks to the development of the whole person in human and Christian virtues (c. 652). Those who govern are obliged to care for the whole person—physically, spiritually and emotionally (c. 619), and institutes must supply their members with all that is necessary according to their own laws for pursuing their vocation (c. 670). And because this consecration involves the whole person, the law also requires some separation—or inviolable privacy, if you will—both material (c. 667) and spiritual (cc. 607, 630) for every member of any institute.

Public Vows

In religious institutes consecration of the whole person is by vow (cc. 607, 654), that is by a free and deliberate promise made to God (c. 1191) through the mediation of the ecclesially approved institute (c. 576) with legitimately designated superiors (cc. 617, 622, 625). The vows must be public, that is recognized by the Church as such (c. 1192), perpetual—or equivalently so (c. 607) and encompass chastity (c. 599), poverty (c. 600) and obedience (c. 601). The vow of chastity includes the obligation of perfect continence in celibacy: the vow of poverty, the obligation of dependence and limitation in the use of goods: and the vow of obedience, the submission of will to legitimate superiors when commanding according to the constitutions.

Ecclesially Approved Institute

Juridical approbation or founding of an institute of consecrated life is within the competence of a diocesan bishop—having consulted the Apostolic See—or of the Apostolic See alone (c. 579). It should be noted that such canonical recognition, or recognition with legal effects in the public arena of the Church, is usually not the initial step in the evolution of an institute. History indicates that more often than not a person or group of persons is first inspired by the gospel message in such a way that the response spearheads renewed devotion to the Good News. This then seems to attract others who desire somehow to share in the inspiration or vision and consequently contribute their efforts to the visible manifestation of this response. Ecclesial approbation is not there creating the inspiration at the outset, but it does create a juridical entity with certain rights and obligations once such approbation has been eventually sought and received (c. 576).

Consequences of Approbation

One might say, legally speaking, that ecclesial recognition of a religious institute, somewhat like the consequences of marriage, is a "package" deal. Upon approbation a religious institute automatically becomes what is canonically referred to as a "juridic person," somewhat comparable to a civil corporation. It is governed by cc. 113–123 on juridic persons and automatically has certain rights and obligations in the Church. Some of the more important ones for religious institutes are the right to continued existence and internal autonomy according to law (cc. 120, 584, 586), the right and obligation to have duly approved proper law (cc. 587, 595), the right to own, administer and sell property (c. 634) and the obligation to conduct all business regarding that property in accord with church law (c. 635). Two other consequences of juridic personality for religious institutes are a limited format for internal structures and public incorporation in the local and universal church.

Among other requirements at present the legal format of religious life includes common life (c. 607). At the very least this means members of the same institute must have a common law or rule with a common supreme internal superior. Common life also obliges communities of religious and individual members to live in houses of the institute sharing some sort of familial life beneficial to the group (cc. 608, 665). Identifiable legitimately constituted superiors who have personal authority by reason of their office as defined in the proper law of the institute, whether elected or appointed, are also required (cc. 608, 626). The personal authority of legitimate superiors is limited by law (cc. 596, 617) as well as by the requirement for each institute to hold periodic general chapters with legislative power (c. 631) and for each superior to have a council whose advice or consent must be obtained in various matters according to the norm of universal and proper law (c. 627).

The consequences of ecclesial approbation incorporating any institute publicly into the local church (or diocese) and into the universal Church are primarily related to the exercise of the apostolate. The first norm in the canons regarding apostolate states that the primary apostolate of all religious—whether active or contemplative—is the witness of consecrated life (c. 673). The next two norms refer to the hidden fruitfulness of prayer and holiness specific to contemplative institutes (c. 674) and to the spiritual source of all apostolic works in active institutes (c. 675). Because institutes are members of the worldwide, visible ecclesial body of the Church, institutes and their members are ultimately subject to the Apostolic See and to the Roman Pontiff as their highest ecclesiastical authorities (c. 590). Because institutes and members also live and serve within some particular church or diocese, they are likewise subject to the diocesan bishop in all matters in which he is competent by reason of his office—such as the care of souls, operating of schools and hospitals, matters of divine worship and the like (cc. 678, 683). The diocesan bishop in consultation with the legitimate superiors of the institutes concerned should foster an ordered cooperation among the various groups and persons who aid in the apostolic works of the diocese (c. 680), and there should be appropriate written agreements regarding the carrying out of such works (c. 681).

Summary of the Essentials

Perhaps at this point the assessment of the essentials of religious life as contained in the new code and as mentioned above bears repetition, namely:

> Religious life is a way of life that consists in following Christ with consecration of the whole person by means of public vows in an ecclesially approved institute which results in certain structures and a definite incorporation into the local and universal church.

Obviously the intention of the law is not to dictate or to define the reality of religious life. Rather it is to follow and to flow from that life which has been an integral part of the Church since the early centuries and which has historically been manifest in certain patterns (i.e., common life and superiors) with the evolutionary addition of certain structures (i.e., councils and general chapters) and with different patterns of ecclesial incorporation (i.e., pontifical and diocesan).

Perhaps at this point it might also be useful to recall the

purpose, functions and limits of law as mentioned in the previous chapter. The law is there to indicate certain fundamental structures, to articulate basic rights and obligations, and to require indispensable procedures. The "package deal" regarding religious institutes, in fact, does just that. But the "package deal" of universal law cannot delineate the exact nature of any religious institute which is precisely why numerous canons of the general law require further explicitation in the proper law of each institute. Note well, however, that the proper law of any institute and both the universal and proper law taken together cannot possibly capture the charism of a particular institute. Charisms live in people, not in codes or constitutions or directories—however finely polished and legally sound. The charism of an institute lives in its members, or it simply does not live at all.

Likewise, recall that a primary function of law is much like that of a skeleton—it should provide a solid basis from which a living entity can exist and grow and evolve. But any skeleton also includes structural and mobile limitations. Human persons are bound by their internal combinations of joints which make it difficult for most people to bend over backwards or to stand on their heads. The legal skeleton of religious institutes is much the same in that it perceives religious life as consisting of specific components, some of which can be dispensed with upon occasion, but most of which are currently considered basic and thus limit the structure and mobility of any religious institute within its legal context. The proper law specification of items in universal law allows each institute to diversify its legal articulations within certain boundaries while providing for the practice of conciliar principles of subsidiarity, collegial action and participative involvement.

Finally, recall again that canon law is a human instrument formulated and implemented by human beings in a thoroughly human milieu. That is not to deny the divine element of the

Church in any aspect of its legal manifestations. Rather, it openly faces the reality that the human element of the Church is always undeniably and rightfully there. To ignore the truly human dimension of the Church—while causing innumerable day to day problems—in some way also denies or renders less efficacious the self-emptying of Jesus who thought it not unworthy to become truly human with all that this entails.

DIAGRAM I

Code of 1917,	Book II Persons	cc. 87–725
Part I	Clerics	cc. 108–486
Part II	Religious	cc. 487–681
Title IX	Institutes, Provinces, Houses	cc. 492–498
Title X	Government	cc. 499–537
Title XI	Admission	cc. 538–586
Title XII	Studies for Religious Clerics	cc. 587–591
Title XIII	Obligations and Privileges	cc. 592–631
Title XIV	Transfer	cc. 632–636
Title XV	Departure	cc. 637–645
Title XVI	Dismissal	cc. 646–672
Title XVII	Societies of Common Life	cc. 673–681
Part III	Laity	cc. 682–725
Code of 1983,	Book II The People of God	cc. 204–746
Part I	The Christian Faithful	cc. 204–329
Part II	Hierarchical Constitution of the Church	cc. 330–572
Part III	Institutes of Consecrated Life and Societies of Apostolic Life	cc. 573–746
Section I	Institutes of Consecrated Life	cc. 573–730
Title I	Common Norms	cc. 573–606
Title II	Religious Institutes	cc. 607–709
Ch. 1	Houses	cc. 608–616
Ch. 2	Government	cc. 617–640
Ch. 3	Admission	cc. 641–661
Ch. 4	Obligations and Rights	cc. 662–672
Ch. 5	Apostolate	cc. 673–683
Ch. 6	Separation	cc. 684–704
Ch. 7	Religious who are Bishops	cc. 705–707
Ch. 8	Conferences of Major Superiors	cc. 708–709
Title III	Secular Institutes	cc. 710–730
Section II	Societies of Apostolic Life	cc. 731–746

Chapter 5
The "Old" and "New" Faces of the New Code

We have seen that law follows life and does not dictate or create reality. Thus it should be no surprise that the "new" code is perhaps 80 to 90 percent "old." Basically it uses material from the 1917 code, from subsequent legislation and practice, from Vatican II documents and from the interim legislation—or *ius vigens*—since the council. In order to understand the newness and oldness more clearly, let us look first at some similarities and differences in the general format of the canons, then at the specific categories of canons within that general format and at the *ius vigens* immediately prior to promulgation of the 1983 code. Finally, let us look at some major changes from the *ius vigens* to the current code.

General Format

For the most part the canons of the 1917 code dealing with religious institutes and the comparable canons of the 1983 code are presented in the same sequence which can be generally summarized as:

1. What is this canonical entity and how is it organized and governed?
2. How does one become a member of a religious institute (i.e., how does one get in)?

3. What are the rights and obligations of members?
4. How does one cease to be a member of a particular institute by transfer or departure (i.e., how does one get out)?

Both codes are divided into "books" which are subdivided into "parts" which are subdivided into "sections." Sections are groupings of consecutive "titles" which are subdivided into "chapters," and these are subdivided into "articles." Articles are groupings of consecutive "canons." And canons are the smallest integral and most easily located unit of each code. Thus "canon" is the term ordinarily used to refer to some portion of the law in either code. However, looking at the organization of the successive subdivisions of the two codes—which are simply listed in Diagram I (p. 42) for the sake of both brevity and clarity in comparison—some notable changes are immediately evident.

Note that in the former code clerics come before religious who come before laity in Book II entitled "Persons." In the latter, the Christian faithful—of whom some are members of the clergy and some are members of institutes of consecrated life—come first in Book II now entitled the "People of God." The 1917 code format was patterned on the basic divisions of Roman law and reflected a highly hierarchical constitution of the Church as understood at the turn of the century. The 1983 code format is patterned on the basic divisions of Vatican II's *Lumen gentium* and reflects a communal as well as hierarchical notion of the Church.

Specific Categories

Note within the format that "consecrated life"—or more specifically, "life consecrated by profession of the evangelical counsels"—rather than "religious" is now the basic category. Looking more closely, note that a new entity called "secular institutes," which were first given universal law approbation in 1947 and subsequently mentioned in *Perfectae caritatis,* is now included as a form of consecrated life. Some norms—thirty-four in fact—are common to both religious and secular institutes. There are now only 103 canons referring specifically to religious institutes which number, combined with the common norms, is still about forty less than the number of canons previously applicable to religious as such.

The former code had a section on the training of religious who are clerics, which canons are now more appropriately contained in the section on clerics. The new code includes eleven canons on the apostolate, while this topic was previously entirely omitted as a section. There is also in the new code the addition of a few canons on conferences of major superiors, which began to form in the 1950s and 1960s and were mentioned specifically in *Perfectae caritatis.* Notable for their brevity in the 1983 code are the twenty-one canons on separation—comprising transfer, exclaustration, departure and dismissal. The 1917 code contained twenty-seven canons on the topic of dismissal alone.

The Ius Vigens

As previously mentioned, the *ius vigens*—or law that is currently flourishing and in practice—is important because it provides an ongoing example of the principle that law actually does follow life. Those who have lived through the two decades of transition since Vatican II know all too well that the *ius vigens* for religious changed rapidly and extensively during those years. For some it was an exciting time of bold experimentation and great expectations. For others it was a trying time of shattering ancient myths and questioning revered values. For many, if not all in religious life, the era of adaptation and renewal has not yet been concluded. On the one hand, the more demanding internal renewal required for genuine new life in institutes is still "catching up" to the external adaptation that occurred swiftly with often polarizing and alienating results. On the other hand, consecrated life in the Church is itself still in an era of evolution and transition with new forms of common life, authority structures and apostolate emerging. It is safe to say, however, that no member of any institute could have remained untouched by the directives and subsequent innovations of Vatican II. Interim legislation is listed in the following table.

INTERIM LEGISLATION

Abbreviation	Document
AI	*Ad instituenda*
CA	*Cum admotae*
CD	*Christus Dominus*
CS	*Cum superiores*
DC	*Dum canonicarum*
DP	*Deserunt praebendo*
ES	*Ecclesiae sanctae*
LG	*Lumen gentium*
PC	*Perfectae caritatis*
PI	*Processus iudicialis*
PM	*Pastorale munus*
RC	*Renovationis causam*
RE	*Regimini ecclesiae*
RL	*Religionum laicalium*
VS	*Venite seorsum*

The following summary of interim legislation, roughly that from the beginning of Vatican II to the present, is not an attempt to concretize history from a chronological legal perspective, since history itself is much more a qualitative than chronological reality and since a merely legal perspective can never capture the whole story. But certain juridical events, events with consequences in church law, have occurred since 1963 which are significant for a better understanding of the new code. Some of the more important of these juridical events are explained here briefly using the date, the *incipit* (or first two words of the original Latin text), the type of document, its source, and some of its more relevant content as related to the present law in order to help the reader understand recent canonical evolution regarding religious life. Because such a summary could be more canonically tedious and lengthy than is desirable for the uninitiated reader, some of the documents are explained with greater detail in Appendix III.

November 30, 1963, *Pastorale munus* [PM], *motu proprio* (i.e., papal legislation) by Paul VI. This granted certain faculties (power to act in areas previously restricted) and privileges (special favors perpetual in nature) to local ordinaries (diocesan bishops and those comparable in law). Items of PM pertaining to cloister, transfer, and dismissal from a diocese are now contained in cc. 667, 679 and 684.

November 6, 1964, *Cum admotae* [CA], pontifical rescript (i.e., written reply) by the papal Secretariat of State. This granted faculties, most of which were to be used with the consent of their council, to the heads of clerical pontifical religious institutes and to abbots president of monastic congregations in response to petitions made by persons in these positions. Faculties concerning dispensation from vows, absence from the house, and renunciation of patrimony are reflected in cc. 665, 668 and 688 of the new code.

November 21, 1964, *Lumen gentium* [LG], dogmatic constitution of Vatican Council II. Chapter VI, ##43–47, of this document deals with "religious" after having dealt in previous chapters with the hierarchical constitution of the Church and the universal call to holiness. Its affirmation of the evangelical counsels can be found in cc. 573–575 and numerous other canons of the new code, while the ecclesiastical approbation and regulation mentioned in LG ##43–47 are reflected in cc. 576–578, 590–591, 678 and other new canons.

October 28, 1965, *Christus Dominus* [CD], decree of Vatican Council II. CD##33–35 in particular greatly affected the notion of exemption (or the privilege of more or less not being subject to the jurisdiction of the diocesan bishop), and this is clearly incorporated in cc. 674 and 678–683 of the new code.

October 28, 1965, *Perfectae caritatis* [PC], decree of Vatican Council II. PC, perhaps more than any other document before or since, is responsible for the impetus and direction of the recent changes in religious life. Consequences of its articulations are found specifically in cc. 573, 578, 587, 599–602, 607–608, 619, 630, 640, 652, 659, 661–665, 669, 673–675, 677 and 708–709. Its attitudinal approach to religious life is the foundation for many of the other canons as well as some of the format of the new code. In short, a familiarity with this document gives one an instant familiarity with both the tone and much of the content of the present code. Its influence on the renewal and subsequent legislation can probably only be underestimated.

May 31, 1966, *Religionum laicalium* [RL], faculties by the Sacred Congregation for Religious. This grant of faculties was similar to that of CA but directed to the heads of pontifical lay religious institutes. It primarily affected the same matters and canons as mentioned under CA.

August 6, 1966, *Ecclesiae sanctae* [ES], *motu proprio* by Paul VI. Part I, ##22–40, or ES implemented the comments of CD##33–35 (q.v., above) and Part II in its entirety, ##1–

The "Old" and "New" Faces of the New Code 49

44, implemented the comments of PC (q.v., above). The document was more or less a set of legal directives on how to go about renewing religious life according the vision of Vatican II. Although its comments do not appear directly in the new code, its plan for implementation of CD and PC set the stage for much of what is actually contained in the current law.

August 6, 1967, *Regimini ecclesiae* [RE], constitution by Paul VI. This document reorganizing the Roman Curia, or the staff and departments of the Apostolic See that aid the pope in governing the universal Church, and changed the former Sacred Congregation for Religious into the Sacred Congregation for Religious and Secular Institutes [SCRSI] with two divisions, one for each type of institute mentioned in the title. It is basically this congregation to which canons such as 579, 582–584, 593, and others are referring when they contain the term "Apostolic See."

January 6, 1969, *Renovationis causam* [RC], instruction by SCRSI. Although instructions are generally nonlegislative directives to help carry out other laws, this instruction—as was clear from its content if not from its title—actually revised the entire section of the 1917 code regarding formation. Its articulations appear, with some alterations, in the new cc. 607, 646–649, 654, 655, 657 and 690.

November 27, 1969, *Cum superiores* [CS], decree by SCRSI. CS, at the request of many superiors to whom the matter pertained, enlarged one faculty of RL (q.v., above) so that heads of pontifical lay religious institutes could, in effect, release from vows those in temporary profession without having recourse to the local ordinary. This form of the faculty—for the head of any institute, clerical or lay—is now contained in c. 688.

June 4, 1970, *Ad instituenda* [AI], faculties by SCRSI. This grant of faculties altered several requirements of the 1917 code with a view to facilitating experimentation and allowed, among other things, delay in drawing up a will until prior to perpetual profession. This was incorporated in c. 668 of the new code.

December 8, 1970, *Dum canonicarum* [DC], decree by SCRSI. Part I of this decree did away with the 1917 code requirement for special confessors for all religious houses and for special jurisdiction in order for priests to hear validly the confessions of religious women. These alterations, which still required appointment of confessors for special cases such as cloisters and formation houses, are now contained in c. 630. Part II of this decree, which allowed the exclusion from renewal of vows or from perpetual profession in specialized situations of sickness contracted after first profession, was included—again with some alteration—in c. 689.

January 30, 1970, *Deserunt praebendo* [DP], directives by SCRSI. This private reply issued in the form of a decree indicated the obligation in charity, justice, equity, and social responsibility of institutes to provide assistance for members who had departed. While reaffirming the principle that former members can make no financial claim for previous services rendered, c. 702 of the new code includes reference to the obligations of justice and charity mentioned in DP.

March 2, 1974, *Processus iudicialis* [PI], decree by SCRSI. The several processes of dismissal for the several different categories of institutes as contained in the 1917 code were basically suppressed by this decree so that one simplified process then in use was applied to all dismissal procedures. This simplified but specific procedure was incorporated into cc. 697–700 of the new code.

Before terminating this treatment of the *ius vigens,* note that most of the above documentation appeared in the decade immediately following the convocation of Vatican II. With rare exception—one such possibly being the 1981 raising to one million dollars of the monetary limit for alienation of (i.e., selling or otherwise encumbering) ecclesiastical property—there simply were no major legislative enactments in the decade from 1974 to promulgation of the new code. This is not to say that there were no significant individual replies and decisions, which legally concerned only those to whom they were directed, during this time. Nor is it to suggest that other nonlegislative documents—such as "Mutual Relations" (78), "Religious and Human Promotion" (80) or "The Contemplative Dimension of Religious Life" (80) are to be summarily ignored. It is rather to call attention to the fact that the current code—incorporating as it does so much post-Vatican II legislation—is not only not very new but is in many ways, and certainly by contemporary evolutionary standards, perhaps much older than one would ever suspect.

Major Changes

Given the numerous already existing norms contained in the 1983 code, one might logically ask what, if anything, is actually new? In fact, in addition to the post-Vatican II mindset and format, there are many alterations of varying significance in the canons on religious. Looking sequentially into these canons of the 1983 code, the more significant changes in actual content from the *ius vigens* can be readily identified. Some of these are summarized here for the general information of the reader.

In the "Common Norms" (cc. 573–606) there is no longer a lengthy canon (1917 code c. 488) defining "order," "congregation," "nun," "formal house," etc.; and the canon on precedence (1917 code c. 591) has been deleted. The internal division of any institute now is within the competence of the institute's internal authorities according to proper law (1983 code c. 581), whereas this had been restricted to the Apostolic See for pontifical groups (1917 code c. 494). The categorization of an institute as "clerical" or "lay" now depends on the intention of the founder or foundress, or on the assumption by the institute of the exercise of sacred orders as recognized by church authority (1983 code c. 588). Formerly, this distinction was numerical, that is dependent on whether the members for the most part were clerics or not (1917 code c. 488#4). For diocesan institutes, now only the bishop of the place where the principal house is located must approve and confirm changes in constitutions (1983 code c. 595), whereas this was formerly the right of the ordinary of any place in which the institute had a legitimate house (1917 code c. 495). Finally, in this title the new code includes hermits and the order of virgins, neither of which was mentioned in the 1917 code as a type of consecrated life (1983 code c. 604).

Regarding government, the lengthy canon of directives for elections—with distinctions for different types of institutes—has been deleted (1917 code c. 506). The supreme moderator of any institute must be designated by a canonical election (i.e., following cc. 164–179 of the new code), and the diocesan bishop is now competent only to preside at such elections for diocesan institutes and some monasteries (1983 code c. 625). An entire chapter of the 1917 code concerning confessors and chaplains, formerly contained under government, has been deleted. The 1983 code simply incorporates the *ius vigens* of DC into one long canon (c. 630) and includes a canon on chaplains for religious (c. 567) in the article concerning chaplains as such (which is no longer contained in the canons on consecrated life).

In the canons of the new code concerning temporal goods of institutes (cc. 634–640), a general requirement is made that all institutes follow the norms of Book V, The Temporal Goods of the Church. This, however, includes c. 1280 containing the new requirement that all public juridic persons have either a finance council or at least two persons who offer advice in financial matters according to the proper law of the juridic person.

There are several major changes in the canons regarding admission to a religious institute. First, there is no longer any postulancy required (1983 code c. 641), but it is the responsibility of the competent superiors to see that only appropriate persons are admitted (1983 code c 642). Second, there is no longer a list of items which render admission either "illicit" or "invalid" (1917 code c. 542). This has been simplified to one short canon on invalidating requirements (1983 code c. 643). Among these the minimum age is now seventeen, the concealment of an illness has been deleted, and concealment of incorporation into another institute of consecrated life or a society of apostolic life has been added as invalidating. Third, regarding novitiate, the contents of RC have generally been included in cc. 647–649—but with the exclusion of various time requirements, except for the minimum twelve months and maximum two years. Fourth, with respect to profession, eighteen is now the minimum age for validity for first vows, with twenty-one for perpetual vows; and perpetual profession may be anticipated by as much as three months (1983 code cc. 656, 658). Fifth, profession in a religious institute must be by public vow (1983 code cc. 607 and 654), with the RC possibility of "promises" now excluded. Finally, the former distinction between the legal consequences of "simple" and "solemn" vows (1917 code c. 579) is not contained in the canons of the 1983 code regarding religious, although the basic notion of these two types of vow is still included in the section on "Other acts of Divine Worship" in Book IV (c. 1192).

A notable change in the obligations and rights of religious is a shift in responsibility for seeing that basic obligations are fulfilled from superiors (1917 code c. 595) to the members themselves (1983 code cc. 662–664). Likewise, the former general inclusion of religious under all the obligations of clerics (1917 code c. 592) has been reduced to include only a few of those to which clerics are bound (1983 code c. 672).

Several major changes also occur in the general category of "separation." Transfer to another religious institute is now under the auspices of the internal authority of the institutes concerned, and a new novitiate is not required (1983 code c. 684). Exclaustration for up to three years can now be obtained from the supreme moderator of an institute with the consent of council, and "imposed exclaustration"—a practice which has been in effect for over thirty years—appears for the first time in universal legislation in c. 686 of the new code. The effects of exclaustration, whether requested or imposed, are slightly altered with the member's remaining under the care of both the superiors of the institute and the local ordinary and with the possibility of the member's retaining the habit of the institute unless the indult of exclaustration indicates otherwise (1983 code c. 687). Nonadmission to renewal of vows or to perpetual profession for those who become ill after first profession is slightly altered from DC and now requires that the restricting illness was not contracted on account of work in or negligence of the institute itself (1983 code c. 689). The possibility of returning to the same institute after legitimate departure without being required to repeat the novitiate is no longer restricted in c. 690 to those who were in temporary vows as in RC. Finally, although it appears quite different from and is certainly much shorter than the 1917 code norms, the dismissal procedure contained in cc. 697–700 is basically a combination of PI and policies used by SCRSI for the last decade. The exception here is that the decree now automatically takes effect when the member is notified unless the person specifically rejects it at that time (1983 code c. 700).

At the conclusion of these lengthy comparisons, let us recall two comments from previous chapters. First, it is not the purpose of law to be prophetic. Indeed, if law simply manages to provide a stable base for fundamental interrelationships, for basic rights and obligations, for indispensable procedures, and for real life prophets to emerge, it will always be somewhat behind the times. But even from its perspective of "behind the times," law will then have done its mundane job rather well. Second, it is not possible—however "old" or "new" the law appears or is—for those who implement it in the contemporary world and Church to escape the tensions of lived reality. These inevitable tensions can be constructive or destructive depending on one's approach to the entire question of law and its daily application. Some aspects of the current law for religious are certainly more susceptible to giving rise to this tension than others. A few of these possible areas of tension in the interplay of law and religious life—with suggestions for constructive approaches to them—are our next concern.

Chapter 6
Current Practical Concerns

There are day-to-day situations that have canonical connections or ramifications. These situations are dealt with in three areas of constant recurrence. These are common life, obedience and apostolate. Common life includes the notion of houses, or the living circumstances of religious, as well as tbe place of religious superiors. Obedience touches the fundamental meaning of authority in religious life, as well as the role of superiors, chapters, councils, participation and governmental structures themselves. Apostolate is connected to institutional charisms, proper law, adaptation, cooperation, and individual and collective resources, as well as to the local and universal Church and, especially, to the diocesan bishop.

Common Life

The story is told of Pachomius that, after several years of pursuing the ascetical life as a solitary, he had an argument with his brother over the size of a wall they were building as part of some shared habitations for hermits. He realized then that there might be some values in community encounter and in adult dialogue which had escaped him in his "aloneness" and that years of asceticism had in fact left him quite unable to tolerate even a slight difference of opinion in a minor matter. Most religious will recognize in Pachomius' experience the reality of the difficulties in community living which translates—rather inadequately—into the legal category of "common life."

Since there is no definition of common life in either the 1917 or 1983 code, one must look for explanations of the term in canonical commentators. At times, their writings appear to the uninitiated reader as having an overly developed penchant for minute distinctions as well as a finely tuned grasp of the mostly trivial. Remember, however, that canonical commentators merely attempt to explain the law's meaning within the available legal context. Commentators do not make laws and should have no particular vested interest in laws, thus leaving them free to be objective in their explanations. Thoroughness and precision are important insofar as whatever is omitted or whatever is unclear leaves the meaning still obscure. Nevertheless, too much thoroughness and precision leave little room for adjustment and evolution. A happy medium is the commentator's aim, but this is often not easily attained. Such seems to be the case in the remarks concerning common life from commentators on the 1917 code. Most religious would not recognize much of their experience of community living in the canonical explanations of common life.

In the former law common life was a requirement for all religious (1917 code c. 487) and was basically viewed in terms of poverty and place (1917 code cc. 580, 594, 606). The "commonness" of common life had two meanings according to the canonists: (1) belonging to the same juridic person governed by the same rule and superior, and (2) actually dwelling in the same lodging and sharing the same facilities with some other members (minimum 3) of the same juridic person. Only the first meaning was considered essential to religious life, because otherwise solitary ascetics could not belong to the category of "religious" and this would be contrary to the entire history and understanding of religious life as such. In indices to the old code the Latin term *communio* gave a long list of canons on the Eucharist, and the Latin term *communitas* referred one to the terms for custom, interdict, persons, privileges, superiors and suspension. In the new law common life is a requirement for all religious (1983 code c. 607) and is viewed as a means of help and a sign of reconciliation (1983 code c. 602) as well as a place for "religious community" of which Christ in the Eucharist is the center (1983 code cc. 608, 665). The two distinctions formerly made concerning the meaning of the term are probably equally as applicable to the new code as they were to the old. But in indices now available for the 1983 code, the terms community, common life, and religious community can be found and refer the reader directly to canons in the section on consecrated life. Though common life appears to be more emphasized in the new law, the question "Whatever happened to common life?" is often heard among religious. On the other hand the comment "I never want to go back to the way we used to live!" seems just as frequent. Persons making such remarks might often be talking about very different aspects of the common life experienced, but they do offer a practical example of the law's inherent inability to completely or accurately circumscribe the past or present realities of religious life.

The ideas of sharing prayer and the same spirit, of being united in heart and soul, and of bearing one another's burdens—although certainly not original at Vatican II—appear with great emphasis under the topic of common life in PC #15. The new law translates this for any institute into a family modality in which there is a certain communal spirit (1983 code c. 602). Specifically for religious, this means a life in common which is considered part of the basic description of religious life (1983 code c. 607). Religious communities must live in a legitimately established house—which should have a chapel for celebration and reservation of the Eucharist—under the authority of a duly designated superior (1983 code c. 608).

Individual members, including superiors, are expected to live in a religious house (1983 code cc. 629, 665).

The law does not indicate exactly what a religious house is but does carefully circumscribe how one can be legitimately established, altered and suppressed (1983 code cc. 609–612, 616). It also considers such legitimately established religious houses as public juridic persons (1983 code c. 634). One might be tempted to think that, because of changes in apostolates and living circumstances, there are now many religious in the United States who do not live in legitimately established religious houses. In point of fact, most of the houses in which religious have lived in this country since the turn of the century were not legitimately established "religious houses" according to canon law. They were usually residences attached to other entities such as schools or parishes or hospitals and were not separate juridic persons in themselves. It will probably continue to be the case that most religious in this country do not live in religious houses in the strict legal sense, because it would simply not be possible—nor is it necessarily desirable—to change all regular residences of religious into houses of this or that religious institute. But to read into this the suggestion that it does not matter how or where any religious lives is simply a gross misinterpretation of the law. Proper interpretation of any law requires looking behind the letter to the values that are being upheld by this particular legal articulation. Clearly, community, as somehow involving living together and sharing resources on a practical level, is the solid Christian value motivating the new code's approach to common life. This value can be violated by religious living in one or many very large canonically legal "houses," as well as by individual religious living dispersed in numerous apartments or single dwellings. It is also possible that small groups of religious living in many noncanonical residences might be putting the real meaning of the law into practice quite well. Neither of the two meanings of common life, according to the commentators, really tells us much about "community," and none of the canons make living in community be what it is. Recall the external nature of legal norms and how they can serve the People of God if they do not attempt to create or dominate mysteries. In considering how the canons on common life ought to be implemented, there is an ancient rule of law contained in the Decretals which aptly fits here: One who acts according to the letter of the law but contrary to the intention of the law is really breaking the law.

Along the same lines, note that the law does not say every house must have a superior but that every religious community must have a superior and that every superior must live in a house (1983 code cc. 608, 629). Houses are collections of things, while communities are associations of people. The requirement that people in religious communities have legitimately designated superiors is intended to manifest and protect two fundamental values: (1) if the vow of obedience means anything in religious life practically speaking, then it is unrealistic to expect the single head of any sizeable institute to be the direct superior of all its members or groups of members, and (2) if the role of religious superior in the best sense as conceived canonically is to be responsibly fulfilled, then absentee superiors ought not to be the general order of the day. These values are directly connected to our next topic of concern.

Obedience

Obedience in religious life is correlative to authority, and authority in religious life is based—as is the concept of law—on the understanding and explanation of medieval theology and philosophy, especially that of Thomas Aquinas. In this context, religious authority has a teleological orientation, a hierarchical derivation and a personal modality.

Recall that Paul refers to Christ as the **telos nomou** or end of the law. Using the same etymological source, a teleological orientation simply means that people are perceived as acting toward goals or with some destination in mind. Obviously there are various means and various aids available for attaining one's end. Aquinas saw the ultimate goal of all persons as happiness in the presence of God—a worthy objective for anyone in any age it would seem. Aquinas also suggested two fundamental means to help attain this end: (1) an internal means of Grace—which is the free gift of God and (2) an external means of law—which indicates reasonable norms of action for free, intelligent, responsible people. In this context authority is basically the ability to exert influence on the total person as acting toward morally good ends. Thus, God *is* authority. He alone can impinge, if you will, on the totality of our being directing us toward goodness. Anyone else merely *has* authority. Moreover, anyone has it only insofar as he or she shares prudentially in the providence of God. Such prudential participation involves carefully examining the elements of any situation, intelligently judging the moral value of an action, and responsibly deciding to act. Properly examining, judging and acting depend—at least in part—on experience, maturity, knowledge, reasoning, intuition, foresight, caution and care for those concerned.

Having authority as described above is obviously related to its source and that is what constitutes religious authority as hierarchical or divided into different, graded levels. The source of religious authority cannot be in this or that person or group of persons, because all people are of equal dignity in the Christian dispensation. In fact, there is authority within the Christian community, however, precisely because of the dignity of baptized individuals who even naturally form a society. But the language of the law seems to assert that all the authority for religious community comes from official approbation or insertion into the official structure. In this context the source of religious authority appears as somewhat extrinsic, or outside of any particular human being, and is ultimately traced to God—which is also in keeping with the sacramental source of Christian personhood. Such authority is derived hierarchically by possessing a particular position in the ecclesial structure or by being delegated—with higher levels eventually extending to lower levels but with no lower one ever having more authority than its source.

Finally, religious authority has a personal modality, because rightly understood it is exercised only by people, not by things. It is people who can examine, judge and make decisions regarding actions. In varying degrees, people are intelligent, have intuition, learn from experience, grow to maturity, exercise caution and care for other people. In short, people participate prudentially in the providence of God by making decisions regarding the means—this or that choice of practical action—to help other people attain morally good ends. Such an idea of authority, which includes seeking out others to help in decisions or even allowing others to make some decisions for us, is not unknown even in secular and civil spheres. People regularly consult and follow the directives of doctors, lawyers, financial advisers and politicians since it is readily recognized that people have varying degrees of expertise in different areas.

Generally speaking, this view of religious authority sees people as choosing, doing and being responsible for what is done as individual persons, not as groups. Repeated replies of SCRSI to questions about structures of authority have indicated that a totally collective form of government is currently unacceptable for religious life. This does not mean that aspects of consultation, participation, subsidiarity and collective decision making are to be ignored. It means that each person in community has the right to be responsible directly to and to deal directly with another person, not some group. It also means that this other person must have legitimately designated and carefully circumscribed authority, which ordinarily is not perpetually possessed. Moreover, this personal exercise of religious authority by individuals does not mean that such exercise is in any way a private affair. It is always to be exercised for the sake of others in the public forum as a matter of service. The service rendered is actually none other than the making of decisions regarding the choice of alternative means. The one rendering the service is supposed to have or to seek appropriate help in order to make the best decisions for the good of all. And he or she is ultimately responsible—not just to the people, but also to God—for the service rendered.

As mentioned above, religious obedience is the correlative to religious authority. It is precisely through the vow of obedience that any member of any religious institute has already consented—by an intelligent and free decision and by a responsible action—to certain already acknowledged goals and certain already chosen means. In addition, by the "package deal" of current canonical structures in religious life, the vow of obedience gives other legitimately designated specific people the right to make at least some other carefully circumscribed legitimate decisions. The one who has freely and responsibly vowed obedience in an ecclesially approved institute is bound to submit to these legitimate decisions of legitimate superiors when they exercise their authority according to law. This is because—again according to the canonical commentators—the vows made to God through the mediation of an ecclesially approved religious institute result in a type of contract between the member and the institute. The representatives of the institute may exercise their authority only as indicated in the "by-laws," if you will, of the institute. When they do so, the member has the obligation to obey. But, this understanding of the interplay of religious authority and religious obedience is still not voluntaristic. The values here are not based on the subjective command of someone who wills this or that but on the intrinsic goodness of this or that action in relation to the ultimate goal of the persons involved. If the service of authority is being rendered as it should and if the decisions made contribute to the good of all as they should, then both are worthy of being obeyed objectively speaking. These "ifs" loom large in the context of human fallibility from which all authority is exercised and within which all obedience is operative.

This, of course, does not tell the whole story of religious obedience. In the past, perhaps through a confusion of canon law with moral theology, the vow of obedience was often understood by religious in too extensive a manner as encompassing even the unexpressed anticipated desires of one's superior. This confusion of the "vow" with the supposed "virtue" in the matter of obedience has so often left so many with so much misunderstanding and personal hurt that an exhaustive consideration of the subject is not possible here. But with the above comments in mind, the canonical treatment of authority, obedience, government, and superiors in the 1983 code can be more comprehensible.

It is clear that by virtue of the vow (c. 601) members are bound to submit to legitimate superiors commanding according to the constitutions of the institute. Legitimate superiors include the Supreme Pontiff (1983 code c. 590) as was also the case in the former code (1917 code c. 499). By c. 618 all superiors are to exercise the authority received from God in a spirit of service (which should sound very familiar!). While the same canon gives superiors the right to make binding decisions, it urges them to be docile to the will of God and to remember that all are God's children (since all are in this adventure together and heading for the same goal). Another canon gives superiors numerous responsibilities toward the people entrusted to their care: They are to promote voluntary obedience, to have reverence for the human person, to listen to the members of the institute, to foster cooperation for the good of all, to nourish members with the Word of God, to lead in the celebration of liturgy, to be an example in virtue and in observance and to come to the aid of members who are physically, emotionally or spiritually in need (c. 619). Indeed, such responsibilities are no small order for anyone and might be expected of any member of any institute who is publicly committed to a closer following of Christ. As listed in the canons, these responsibilities of superiors are obviously intended to put into practice a care and concern for the whole person (in the context of the common good) to which every member of any institute has a right. Time and experience have shown that some members inevitably lack some care and concern if such is not the responsibility of some one person. If we were in a perfect world with perfect people (which, indeed, we are not!) and if there were not many examples of just such a lack of care and concern (does not everyone know someone to whom no one, for various reasons, will listen?), then the approach of the code toward superiors could be interpreted as a mere perpetuation of maternal and paternal myths of religious life. In fact, the requirements that communities have superiors (c. 608) and that superiors live in houses (c. 629) certainly have more than a little to do with these responsibilities of superiors and with the right of every member to experience basic Christian values and behavior in religious life. Recall that one of the functions of law is to acknowledge recognized Christian values and note that some such values in religious life are considered as too important not to be included in the law.

In the midst of all the responsibilities of superiors, their authority is carefully circumscribed by law, since time and experience also indicate that authority in the Church has often been misused. Superiors must, with rare exception, have limited terms of office and must have a council whose advice or consent is required in prescribed matters (cc. 624, 627). This reflects the need for varied sources of information to assure better choices in making decisions and for an outside check on possible arbitrary decisions. Perhaps to assure both some experience and some maturity—as well as some stability of commitment—all superiors must be perpetually professed (c. 623).

It is not a responsibility of superiors to make laws. Legislative power is given, however, to general chapters which convene only periodically because new law requires combined vision and effort but should not be an ongoing frequent need. Chapters also have the right to elect the head of the institute following the election norms prescribed in universal and proper law (c. 631). This fulfills the law's function of providing procedures for smooth transitions. In elections and in conferring offices, all involved are urged to keep in mind both God and the good of the institute (c. 626), since the ultimate purpose of any institute and its members is beyond them—both individually and collectively. The possibility for cooperation and participation of all members in different aspects of government is both encouraged and assured by law (cc. 631.3, 632–633), since all members are expected to have a special interest in and responsibility for the common efforts of the institute. Finally, the constitutions of each institute must clearly indicate the rights and obligations (in addition to those of universal law) entailed by membership, and each member who pronounces vows in the institute after appropriate formation is thenceforth responsible for adjusting his or her life according to that commitment (cc. 598, 654).

Perhaps more than enough has been said here about the notions of obedience, authority, superiors and government. No verbal considerations, on paper or among people—and certainly not in law—will alter the reality that the hierarchical notion of authority in fact sometimes conflicts with the communal notion that has been the recent experience of many religious. The two approaches—hierarchical and communal—are not necessarily contradictory. There is in the new law ample room for proper law specification of numerous aspects of the required structures and operational modalities in religious life. If the values underlying the current universal law are recognized and if the positive experience of more participative government is acknowledged, the salient elements of both can be joined into a creative and harmonious union. But such an accomplishment will not occur quickly or without effort, and the law regarding it will always be somewhat behind whatever is accomplished in daily life.

Apostolate

The new code is very clear that the primary apostolate of all religious, whether contemplative or active, is the witness of consecrated life (c. 673). Because the witness of those dedicated entirely to the contemplative life is primarily in a hidden apostolic fruitfulness, members of such institutes may not be required to engage in active apostolates even when there is some necessity (c. 674). This canon probably is more of a protection for contemplative groups of men than it is for contemplative groups of women. Men who are members of strictly contemplative institutes are often also clerics whose sacramental ministry is regularly needed within a diocese. The canon does not forbid them from leaving their monasteries to engage in needed sacramental ministries but limits the ability of the diocesan bishop to require them to do so. Women who are members of strictly contemplative institutes are seldom, if ever, called to the active apostolate and are, in fact, subject to an entirely separate set of regulations regarding cloister (which will be considered in the next chapter). In institutes dedicated to apostolic works, their activity is perceived by the code as having both its origin and goal in union with God. Moreover, all such works are exercised in the name of the Church, through its mandate, and in communion with it (c. 675). Thus, while all apostolic activity of religious is spiritually founded, it is also legally based in the institutional Church. Consequently, in the practical exercise of any apostolic activity related to religious institutes, there are two matters of importance to be considered: charism and jurisdiction.

Charism, which is not a legal term, is difficult both to understand and to describe. Apparently for this reason, references to the "charisms" of institutes which appeared in earlier drafts of the code now use the word "gifts" (c. 577) or phrases like "nature, character, and purpose" (c. 588). By whatever name or phrase one refers to the reality, the "charism"—or nature, purpose, spirit and character of an institute (c. 578)—must somehow be contained in its constitutions which in turn must be approved by competent ecclesiastical authority (c. 587). This same authority also has the right and obligation to interpret the evangelical counsels, to moderate their legal practice and to care for the growth of institutes according to their sound traditions (c. 576). An immediate problem, of course, is that "charisms," by whatever name or phrase one refers to the reality, can never be completely captured in any document because they are like a seed planted by a founder or foundress in one generation and which appears possibly as a very different living and growing entity in the next. Equally problematic is that the understanding of the evangelical counsels, the legal moderation of their practice, and the growth of different institutes has varied widely since the early centuries of the Church. Superiors and members of institutes are given the responsibility for faithfully retaining and prudently accommodating the works, in keeping with the "charism" of the institute, to different circumstances and needs (c. 677). Within the boundaries of the respect that must be afforded the traditions and characteristics of an institute's apostolic activity, all religious are subject to the power of the bishop in the general exercise of any public works of the apostolate in the diocese entrusted to his care—and this power of the bishop is clearly "jurisdiction."

Although its source is debated and although now referred to as the "power of governance" (c. 129), jurisdiction is the subject of numerous canons in the new code (cc. 129–144 etc.). A diocesan bishop—or one who is actually in charge of a given diocese—has, by law, all the power of governance he needs to fulfill his pastoral responsibilities (c. 381). In some circumstances the heads of clerical religious institutes of pontifical right (i.e., founded or approved by the Apostolic See according to c. 589) are comparable to bishops in having and exercising the power of governance (c. 134). Likewise, some institutes can be and are removed (or "exempted") from the jurisdiction of local ordinaries by the Supreme Pontiff (c. 591). These, however, are clerical institutes only: and they—as all others—are still subject to the diocesan bishop in matters of public worship, the care of souls, holding ecclesiastical offices, the visitation of schools, and other spiritual or temporal works of the institute related to the external apostolate, as well as in certain disciplinary matters (cc. 678–679, 682–683). Moreover, the bishop has the responsibility of coordinating all the apostolic works in his diocese and of fostering cooperation among all institutes and persons engaged in these various works (c. 680). All diocesan works entrusted to institutes within his diocese remain subject to the bishop, and he is urged to prepare written agreements for such work (concerning hiring, termination, responsibilities and finances) in collaboration with the competent superiors of the institutes involved (c. 681). These norms illustrate the basic principle of ecclesiastical law that whoever has the responsibility for certain matters also has authority over them and is competent to act in their regard.

Institutes that have a legitimately established house in a diocese automatically enjoy the right, by law, to exercise the works proper to the institute in that diocese (c. 611). However, the works in which any religious of any institute may engage are restricted by c. 672 if it entails some of the prohibitions directed to clerics. Currently, perhaps the best known of these is the exclusion from holding a public office which includes the exercise of civil jurisdiction (c. 285.3). Inappropriate or unbecoming activities, which are not named in the 1983 code as they were in the 1917 code but which would obviously still include such positions as executioners, etc., are to be avoided, as well as are civil and financial involvements that may prove burdensome (c. 285.1,2,3). Likewise, participation in political factions and in governing labor unions is restricted for religious (c. 287). Finally, a religious may not undertake positions which are not in accord with the character of the institute without permission of the legitimate superior (c. 671), and apostolic activity does not exempt a religious from the specific obligations entailed by his or her profession (c. 678). A diocesan bishop may prohibit the member of an institute—even one with a legitimately established house—from remaining in the diocese (c. 679). But he may do so only for a very grave reason (of which he is the judge since he is the one legally competent to act) and only by following a specific procedure.

The interplay of values in the area of apostolate is quite complex, and the complexity is reflected in the legal norms. On the one hand, institutes and members, who were urged by Vatican II to return to the gospel and the spirit of the founder or foundress while simultaneously attending to the signs of the times, are responsible for articulating their mission in constitutions and for exercising and adapting the works proper to their charisms. On the other hand, bishops, who were recognized by Vatican II as true successors of the Apostles with appropriate power in their areas of responsibility, are given greater authority over and control of apostolic activities within their care. Again, on the one hand, some of the historically conditioned circumstances in which new institutes were founded no longer exist, and expression of the original purpose must be adapted if these groups are to continue in meaningful service of the Church. Whereas, on the other hand, many areas of service perceived in a former era as extrinsic—such as action on behalf of justice—are now considered by the bishops themselves as "constitutive" of the gospel. On the one hand, the personal and collective resources of some institutes simply no longer permit continuation of former apostolic activities. On the other hand, there is probably no diocese anywhere in which the needs for various corporate and spiritual works of mercy are not increasing and the responses in various apostolic activity to meet these needs are not expanding.

There simply are no panaceas, legal or otherwise, to circumscribe fully the interrelationships between and among bishops and religious institutes and their members. Members of the hierarchy should beware lest they—while interpreting, moderating, approving and caring (c. 576)—exert a stifling influence on genuine works of the Spirit among the People of God. Members of institutes should beware lest they—while witnessing, participating, exercising and adapting (cc. 673, 675–677)—exert a splintering effect on Christian values as institutionally expressed. All must beware lest personal rather than gospel objectives become primary concerns.

Continuing Concerns

It would be well to note here that nothing without a sound basis in reality usually survives very long and that nothing with a sound basis in reality can be totally ignored forever. It would also be well to note here that the institutional church tends to evolve very slowly and legal structures evolve even more slowly. Legal changes are not often made because people—however numerous or vociferous—advocate one or another new position or idea. They are made because time-tested experience in a broad ecclesial base has first altered the practical reality of day-to-day life, and whatever is being done is actually seen as successful without violating already acknowledged values. Reducing common life to having the same letters after one's name or to being on a list for the same residence will scarcely enhance the values underlying the new law about community. Reducing obedience to acceptance of an occasional assignment or reducing authority to ratification of popular opinion will never find a basis in church law because such actions fall so far short of the values the law seeks to protect. Reducing cooperation to an occasional mutual notification of changes in assignment among bishops and major superiors will scarcely further the genuine meaning of apostolic activity. Ignoring the negative effects of past or present misuse of authority or lack of communication or reluctance to adapt will not enhance the exercise of authority or improve communication or promote genuine adaptation. The values people actually experience and which are formative entities in their lives simply cannot be denied. It is not possible, nor is it desirable, to escape the potentially very creative tension of the interplay between spirit and norm. Somewhere between the idea of the Spirit and the reality of law falls the shadow of our very human Church. We live "in between."

Chapter 7
Comments on Cloister for Women

A major change in the 1983 code is its treatment of cloister in comparison to the legislation of the former code. There is now only one canon (c. 667)—as opposed to ten previously (1917 code cc. 597–606)—which even uses the word *clausura*. This numerical distinction can be both revealing and misleading as will be shown later in this chapter. In order to understand the entire concept and legal reality of cloister for women, however, at least some minimal historical explanation of cloister is required.

Evolution of Cloister

The history of cloister for women is basically a chronology of increasing institutional control paralleled by decreasing numerical membership. Different forms of religious life, different types of consecration, and different perceptions of acceptable activity for women developed over the centuries in conjunction with this increasing control of and decreasing membership in cloisters.

The attitude of Jesus toward women as recorded in Scripture is generally accepted as being somewhat better than the treatment afforded them in the prevailing culture. However, some church fathers, especially Jerome and Augustine, often took positions toward women that were ambiguous at best by comparing them to the prototype of Eve as the symbol of sin and temptation or to Mary as the symbol of obedience and salvation. This demanding dichotomy (demanding because most people, women or men, are probably somewhere in between superlative models of evil or good) surfaced strongly in the Middle Ages, as did the long term effects of a consistent lack of opportunity and a static secondary role for women. Cesarius of Arles is known to have written a rule of cloister for women in the early decades of the seventh century, and from that time to the present rules of cloister have always been more strict for women than for men. Justinian, an Eastern civil emperor—roughly a contemporary of Cesarius (see Ch. 2, above), legislated that monks and nuns should not go about the cities but remain in their monasteries (which legislation, incidentally, was regularly quoted by the texts cited in the footnotes to c. 601 of the 1917 code—but was selectively applied only to women).

When the Gregorian reform began in the late eleventh century, most of the legislation that emerged from the subsequent canonist popes was, quite naturally, male in origin and male in character. Thus, the restrictions placed by Lateran IV in 1215 on the founding of new religious orders and the writing of new rules were interpreted for women to mean there could be no other form of religious life than that of cloister with solemn vows. The same restrictions were either subject to exceptions or were legally circumvented for men, however, as the medieval mendicant foundations amply demonstrated. In 1298, Pope Boniface VIII imposed strict cloister with solemn vows as the only acceptable modality of religious life for women and enunciated penalties for anyone who—by allowing other forms or by tampering with this form—violated his legislation. By the beginning of the Renaissance—roughly the mid-fifteenth century—the dichotomy of the early Fathers, the centuries of systematic cultural subordination, the medieval philosophical

Comments on Cloister for Women 77

and theological constructs, and a growing collection of ecclesiastical legislation all converged to a rather severe and strictly applied concept of cloister for women. It was repeated by Trent in 1563 and by Pope Pius v in 1566. Pope Clement vii added more penalties in 1599 (such as the excommunication later incorporated in the 1917 code c. 2342).

After the prohibitions of Trent and subsequent papal legislation had reaffirmed and strengthened previous norms, organizations of men—notably the Jesuits who originated around 1540—managed to receive approbation as religious institutes even though they had no cloister, did not pray choral divine office, claimed no distinctive habit, were exempt from the jurisdiction of the bishop, and were engaging in new areas of apostolic activity. Comparable organizations of women—notably the Ursulines (c. 1535), the Visitation Nuns (c. 1610), the English Ladies (c. 1615) and the Daughters of Charity (c. 1633)—were either suppressed or survived only by adopting cloister and solemn vows or by consciously disassociating themselves from the category of "religious women" as such—since there was obviously only one canonical category available and these groups obviously did not canonically fit into it. Gradually, individual groups of women, some with modified cloister, some with simple or private vows, some with teaching or health-related apostolates, were recognized formally by bishops and then by popes as having quasi-official status in the Church although they did not qualify as "religious" strictly speaking.

In the aftermath of the French Revolution, when ecclesiastical property was confiscated and numerous monasteries were disbanded, those in which some public civil service such as teaching or care for the sick was evident were allowed to remain and retain materials necessary for the services they rendered. This gave impetus to the notions that women could be dedicated to the Church without being cloistered, that they could even engage in external apostolates comparable to those long exercised by men, and that the simple vow (in which personal ownership was retained but use was restricted) could be quite ecclesiastically beneficial. Nevertheless, full papal ecclesiastical recognition of noncloistered women with simple vows and active apostolates was only finally attained through the apostolic constitution *Conditae a Christo* by Pope Leo XIII in 1900. Detailed norms of how such "congregations" (as they were officially called) could obtain approbation, as well as how they were to be structured and governed, were issued shortly thereafter. These turn-of-the-century norms and distinctions, along with the centuries-old articulations regarding cloister, were primarily what became incorporated into canons of the 1917 code.

From the Code to Vatican II

The 1917 code canons directed different regulations regarding cloister to the then different legally defined (in c. 488) categories of religious: to "regulars" (i.e., those in orders with solemn vows)—men or women—in c. 597; to "regulars" who were men, in cc. 598–599; to "nuns" (i.e., women with solemn vows), in cc. 600–603; and to "sisters" (i.e., women in congregations with simple vows), in c. 604. Custody of the cloister was mentioned in 1917 code c. 605. Restricted egress from the cloister was mentioned in 1917 code c. 606. And a rather severe penalty—automatic excommunication (the dispensation of which was reserved, but at the lowest level of such reservation, to the Apostolic See)—applied to violation of the cloister of nuns according to 1917 code c. 2342. Women were not permitted to enter the cloister of men (c. 598): No one was permitted to enter the cloister of women (c. 600). No nun could exit from the monastery (even for a short time under any pretext) without special permission from the Holy See except in danger of death or most grave harm (c. 601). The cloister of nuns was to be so circumscribed that no one could see into it or out of it (c. 602), and the local ordinary was given special vigilance over it—including the power to impose penalties for violations of it (c. 603). There were no similar norms for exit, entrance, or vigilance regarding monasteries of men, monks or otherwise.

In the decade and a half after the promulgation of the 1917 code, two sets of additional norms for cloister were issued by the Sacred Congregation for Religious. The first document, *Nuper edito* issued in 1924, called for strict observance of the new canons and further expounded on their meaning: for example, the windows of monasteries for nuns were to be opaqued so that, indeed, no one would see in or see out; the keys to the cloister, the doors of which were to be locked, should be kept by the superior at all times; those violating the cloister were not only automatically excommunicated but also "guilty of grave sin." This severe legislation led to some of the hair-splitting canonical interpretations of which it has been noted canonists are quite capable, such as incurring the penalty of excommunication if a person took **one step** outside the cloister (or inside, if the person was an outsider) but **only if** this resulted in the person's **entire body** being outside (or inside) the boundaries (*per unum passum, dummodo toto corpore*)! This severe legislation also necessitated subsequent adjustments so that cloistered women could (literally) survive. The second document, *Conditio plurimorum* issued in 1934, actually acknowledged that it was necessary to create a new type of "adjunct nun"—the extern sister—so that the daily physical needs (buying food, caring for the monastery grounds, selling items made by the nuns as a source of income) could be met. These extern sisters were to take simple vows, live outside the cloister and follow a set of rules different from those of the nuns.

The next significant legislation for nuns was the apostolic

constitution *Sponsa Christi* issued by Pope Pius XII in 1950. In it two types of cloister, "major" and "minor," were distinguished with the former referring to 1917 code cc. 600–602 (for "nuns") and the latter referring to 1917 code cc. 599 and 604 (for male "regulars" and for "sisters"). But also in this document, in his explanation of why the new norms were being published, Pope Pius XII noted that "public opinion today will scarcely tolerate too rigorous an interpretation of canon 601." Let the reader recall that he was speaking of the "no exit even for a short time under any pretext" canon of the 1917 code (which had been selectively applied to nuns) and that the comment was uttered more than three decades ago. *Sponsa Christi* represented a distinct change in both the approach toward and the content of previous norms. It was soon followed by additional instructions from the Sacred Congregation for Religious—*Inter praeclara* in 1950, *Inter cetera* in 1956, and *Peculiaris monialium* in 1961—which explained the new legislation and updated the previous norms. These, too, were a great improvement because, although there was still mention of automatic excommunication for the violation of cloister, there was no longer a reference to automatically sinning thereby. It is always a step forward when matters of moral theology (i.e., sin) are recognized as moral theology and not made the subject or object or consequence of a canonical norm.

At the very beginning of Vatican II in late 1963, *Pastorale munus*—with the broad faculty of the bishop regarding cloister in #34—was issued by Pope Paul VI. This faculty, with a slight alteration of wording, has become paragraph four of 1983 code c. 667. *Perfectae caritatis* in late 1965 specifically mentioned the contemplative or the monastic life in ##7, 15, and 16. The document implementing PC, *Ecclesiae sanctae* in 1966, referred to nuns in ##9, 10, 30, 31, and 32. Among the significant legal changes resulting from these documents were that: (1) the constitutions of nuns were to be revised, (2) necessary experiments could be authorized by competent superiors, (3) papal enclosure was referred to as "ascetical" and as a "protection," (4) enclosure was to be adapted but with separation being preserved, and (5) minor cloister was abolished necessitating a choice for all cloistered and semicloistered groups between strict papal cloister or an active apostolic life.

Current Legislation

Canonists and noncanonists alike readily acknowledged that the norms of the 1917 code concerning cloister as applied to women, along with the subsequent legislation and interpretation, were both more extensive and more strict than as applied to men. And, generally speaking, this difference in treatment was accepted by those concerned—men and women—as appropriate to and helpful for their respective legal status and roles. The one canon of the new code dealing directly with cloister is much simpler, having only four paragraphs none of which is very lengthy. But in its very simplicity, c. 667 may both cloak and perpetuate some of the former law's unequal distinctions and underlying presumptions.

In paragraph one, all houses—in the technical sense of "house" and not restricted to monastic houses—are to observe some cloister appropriate to the particular institute as determined in its own law in such a way that some part of the house is always reserved to the members. The Latin term used for members is significant because it refers to both men and women. The stricter cloister to be observed in monasteries dedicated to the contemplative life, according to paragraph two, also applies equally to monasteries of men and of women as is clearly indicated by the Latin words of the official text. But then there are some specific distinctions made among types of monasteries, in paragraphs three and four of this canon and elsewhere, which seem to reintroduce former inequalities.

There are houses of monks (*monachorum*), monasteriess of nuns (*monialium*) and self-governing monasteries (*sui iuris*). The one norm applying to monks (c. 613) says that their houses are automatically self-governing and that the moderators of such houses are automatically major superiors. One of the ten canons concerning self-governing monasteries (c. 1427, in the book on procedures, in the article on judges), obviously refers only to men because it uses the term "abbot." Five of the canons (cc. 625.2, 628.2, 637, 638.4 and 699.2) refer to a special type of self-governing monastery described in c. 615. This is one in which there is no superior extraneous to the monastery who has actual power in the monastery according to its constitutions. In other words, it refers to monasteries which are self-contained units and are not members of another larger "umbrella" group (such as a monastic congregation whose superiors have some authority over the member houses). Since there is, in fact, no intermediate superior between these monasteries and the Holy See, they are committed to the special vigilance of the diocesan bishop by c. 615. This vigilance is further specified by the canons listed above: He presides at the elections of superiors (c. 625.2), he has the right of visitation regarding discipline (c. 628.2), he must be informed annually of the administration of its temporal goods (c. 637), he must give his written consent for the validity of certain administrative acts (c. 699.2). All of these norms seem—and are— eminently reasonable, but they are also circumstantially discriminatory because (in fact) there is rarely a monastery of monks which fits the description of c. 615 and (in fact) there is rarely a monastery of nuns that does not fit it. In addition, two canons are specific restrictions regarding monasteries of nuns: They can be established only with the permission of the Apostolic See (c. 609), and only the Apostolic See can suppress them

(c. 616.4). But the deceptively simple c. 667 remains the most significant one in the new code for nuns.

Paragraph three of c. 667 requires monasteries of nuns which are totally dedicated to the contemplative life to observe "papal cloister" according to the norms of the Apostolic See. Paragraph four reiterates the interim legislation of *Pastorale munus* #34 (see Ch. 5, above) regarding the competence of the diocesan bishop in granting entrance to or exit from the cloister. The *ius vigens* for "papal cloister" is *Venite seorsum,* an apostolic constitution issued by Pope Paul VI on August 15, 1969. It applies only to women and has not been significantly altered by any subsequent legislation, the current code revision notwithstanding. At a first or superficial glance, therefore, it appears that the 1983 code has not made any significant advances in the matter of cloister for women. On the other hand, if the *ius vigens* is interpreted in its proper context of legal and historical evolution, there is a definite difference, even in the light of the above-mentioned and sometimes subtle inequalities that are incorporated in the new code.

Venite seorsum is written in two parts: the first offering a theological and spiritual explanation of the cloistered contemplative form of life for women; the second indicating specific norms for them. In some ways it appears to be a combination—but not a very good mixture—of a newer and more recent attitudinal approach toward papal cloister (of Pope Pius XII and Vatican II) and the former somewhat severe legislation (of the 1917 code and subsequent norms). Part II reaffirms many comments and implications of PC and ES II:

- cloister for nuns should be adapted but must be approved by the Apostolic See (#1);
- the cloister should be circumscribed by some "material separation" which must be defined in the constitutions (##3–4);

- the nuns, novices and postulants must live inside while others must remain outside (##5–6);
- nuns may be absent from the cloister for necessary functions (such as, consulting doctors, doing manual work on monastery grounds, exercising civil rights) with the consent of the superior for as long as one week (#7, b);
- absences not listed or those longer than one week but less than three months may be granted by the local ordinary and beyond three months, by the Holy See (#7, c and d);
- use of communication media (radio, television, newspapers, periodicals) is restricted (##10–11).

Remnants of former legislation are also evident:

- nuns may leave the cloister in the case of serious imminent danger (#7, a)
- those whose skills are necessary (i.e., plumbers, electricians) may enter the cloister (#8, g);
- among those permitted to enter the cloister without special permission are heads of state, their wives and their retinue (#8, b);
- nuns can at times and by way of exception be permitted to attend meetings that really foster the cloistered life (#12);
- departure from and entrance to the cloister must be carefully recorded and this record inspected at the time of canonical visitation (#14).

And, some of the norms are of particular importance in their relation to moral theology and law:

- the law of cloister entails a serious obligation in conscience for all (nuns and non-nuns) (#13);

- penalties for the violation of cloister are without force until the promulgation of the new code (#16).

In the perspective of former years, note that the right of heads of state and their wives and retinue to enter cloisters as affirmed here is certainly not an overriding concern in the twentieth century (#8, a). Note also that sound legal tradition does not usually legislate for cases of extreme necessity or instances (i.e., serious imminent danger) in which common sense should ordinarily suffice (##7, a and 8, g). And there appears to be a presumption that meetings, even gatherings organized specifically for nuns, are suspect at best and at the very least are to be avoided #12).

In the perspective of Vatican II, on the other hand, note that nuns may define the material separation of the cloister in their proper law and that grilles and opaqued windows are no longer a concern of the universal law of the Church (##3-4). Likewise, instances allowing egress from the cloister are less closely circumscribed than previously and provide for the exercise of judgments by those closer to the matter at hand, namely the superior of the monastery and the local ordinary (##7, b and c). The restriction of communication media might appear rather strict (#10-11), but, in fact, it is no more forcefully stated than a comparable norm of the 1983 code (c. 666) which is addressed to all members of religious institutes. Note too that the obligation in conscience for observation of cloister is very well stated and keeps the Church safely out of the dangerous business of legislating sin (#13). Moreover, since penalties for violation of cloister were abolished until the new code (#16) and since the new code has not included any such penalties, there simply no longer are any universal Church law sanctions for the violation of cloister. Thus, matters of conscience are left as matters of conscience and no longer afford opportunities for the "one step, provided the whole body follows" distinctions of some possibly over enthusiastic canonists.

A Deeper Look and Different Words

There are some unarticulated presumptions in the above comments on cloister for women. One is that the cloistered contemplative vocation is especially unique in the Church. This is not to say that any other vocation of any Christian is not unique, but that—given its history and diminished existence—the cloistered contemplative vocation by reason of its very survival must still have something special and unique to offer the People of God. Another presumption, which is really more in the nature of a conclusion based on historical evidence, is that the legislation on cloister for women has been highly influenced by social, cultural, philosophical and theological circumstances and that it has often been applied in an overly severe and possibly unjust manner. A third presumption is that all those in cloisters are not necessarily contemplatives and that not all contemplatives are necessarily in cloisters— whence the very carefully chosen term "cloistered contemplatives" at the beginning of this list of presumptions. The fourth is that the uniqueness of the cloistered contemplative vocation really does require special or different legislation, if you will, in order to help give stability to and guarantee the values of this unique form of consecrated life. The fifth, and last, is that what is needed most at the moment is a new perspective on and a new vocabulary for this cloistered contemplative vocation.

Let us begin these concluding remarks, therefore, by speaking not of "cloister," but of "commitment," and of the "space" needed—indeed, to which one has a right—in order to live one's commitment in consecrated life. All religious are committed to following Christ more closely, not as a matter of legislation but as a matter of personal choice. The law recognizes that all religious need some material and immaterial, individual and collective "space" if we are to carry out and persevere in the commitment made. It may be called "privacy" or it may be called the "inviolability of conscience;" but, by whatever name, it is seen as an indispensable value and is, therefore, addressed in law (cc. 630, 667). It is always better, however, not to begin (or, ultimately, to end) by considering law, but by considering the deeper meanings of the "commitment" and the "space" it requires.

The space required for fulfilling one's commitment in any religious institute, whether of men or of women, depends in part on the person(s) involved and in part on the structures and functions of the institute itself. Franciscans are not organized and do not function in the same manner as Dominicans. Dominicans are equally as distinct in structure and function from Carthusians as they are from Jesuits. Moreover, within each of these recognized groups there is a variety of persons manifesting a variety of personalities with a variety of gifts and needs. The gifts are used and the needs are met by different people in different ways in different institutes. All people in any form of commitment in every walk of life have various means of confronting and of avoiding the task of recognizing and using gifts and recognizing and meeting needs. **Whether** and **how** the Christian confronts or avoids these responsibilities has something to do with **if** and **to what extent** one is transformed into the likeness of Christ, which after all—at least according to Paul—is a primary objective of our lives. Through the centuries it appears that the cloistered contemplative form of religious life has traditionally been structured and has regularly functioned in such a way that, at least **theoretically,** one is presented with the least possible means of avoidance and the greatest possible means of confrontation for transformation into the likeness of Christ. Thus, the cloistered contemplative form of religious life—for men or for women—is automatically and categorically a very demanding choice with very limited built in avoidance mechanisms. And that is precisely why this commitment—because of the type of commitment and the demands it makes with its limited alternatives—requires what we might call "contemplative space." The word "cloister," in addition to being encrusted with centuries of collective and individual misunderstandings, simply limps in conveying the meaning and the importance of this "contemplative space" to the commitment at hand.

Looking at the vocation of cloistered contemplatives from this perspective and in this manner of speaking gives more meaning to many of the norms on cloister for women and renders a few of the otherwise minute ones somewhat understandable. In this context a material separation for their "space" makes eminent sense to ensure the privacy of the physical area in which the commitment is lived. In this context recording entrance and egress is transformed from a check on potential violations of the physical "space" to a valuable running account of how the "space" provided is actually being used—materially and otherwise—for the benefit of all. In this context the norm regarding use of communication media is transformed from a *fuga mundi* admonition to a call for responsible use of the "space" that can be easily and genuinely violated without anyone ever physically crossing its circumscribed limits or its material separation. In this context the responsibility in conscience of all people regarding violations of the "space" to which cloistered contemplatives have a right has its best possible Christian meaning—namely that the law does, indeed, consider the People of God as intelligent and free and that the consequences of any personal choice must be fulfilled by that person but must also be respected by others. Indeed, let us be so bold as to suggest that, in this context, the only norms of papal cloister for women which are not transformed and rendered more understandable are those which—in direct contrast to the treatment of cloistered contemplative men—do not allow women the right to make decisions of which they are fully capable regarding themselves and the use of their own "contemplative space." These simply cannot be transformed, because they appear to be—in reality—the institutionalized perpetuation of a former era's prejudiced perspective regarding the inferiority of women and of their presumed inability to conduct their own affairs in a responsible manner.

At the end of this conclusion, it should be noted that it is very possible that cloistered contemplative women have a unique opportunity for Christian witness in the modern world. They can witness very clearly to the futility of the world's current overproduction, overconsumption, overstimulation, and overactivity which are contrary to the gospel and contribute to the dissipation of energy and to mutual destruction. They can stand in contradiction to the "what-you-see-is-what-you-get" mentality by the witness of lives in which you never really "see-what-you-get" but in which "what-you-get" is far more than anyone can ever really "see." They can witness deeply to the fact that true wealth has to be more than mere money, that true love has to be more than mere sexuality, and that true power has to be more than mere control of others. Perhaps primarily—and in a very special way—they can also witness to the reality that the struggle of humanity to live in God is not a futile struggle after all and that firm hope in the promises of a God who has never not kept his promises is far from an empty hope, indeed.

Chapter 8
Further Cautions, Some Legal Fallacies, and a Few Woes

Further Cautions

After all that has been said to this point regarding canon law and its place in the Church, there are further cautions to be mentioned regarding the various ways in which religious can respond to legal norms. Three basic responses are compliance, identification and internalization. The first is usually (or hopefully) directed toward the numerous, somewhat arbitrary, circumstantially conditioned but helpful norms in religious life, such as the scheduling of meals or community prayers. A compliance response allows appropriate variation in what one would like in such matters since many external factors beyond the control of the religious themselves often affect the final decision more than individual or collective preference (such as the already established school day or the hospital schedule, etc.). It is usually easier and wiser to comply with such decisions acknowledging they may necessitate occasional exceptions and alterations, since—even if minor needs are not met by them—there is a realization that more energy ought not to be expended regarding these matters than the results for one's personal needs or preference actually warrant.

The second form of response, identification, is also basically an external one and fills a somewhat utilitarian purpose. A key function of this response is to help the person "identify" with the values of the rest of the group, or at least with the accepted manifestations of these values by which one can often be recognized as—or feel a sense of—belonging to the group. Values and belonging, however, are not external matters, so decisions in various areas of identification response often require more personal involvement, take more time, and are less easily adjusted. Religious might readily recognize an identification response in the approach toward the community's habit, apostolate, or home base (i.e., "motherhouse"), or even—for contemplatives—the material cloister. These are certainly not in the same value category as daily schedules but also ought not to be in the same category as one's response to norms regarding the object of the vows, for instance.

The third form of response, or internalization, is directed toward those norms which are deeply value-expressive and are only minimally conditioned by historical circumstantces. Any matter afforded an internalization response should be one that has been freely chosen from among various alternatives with full knowledge of the consequences and is put into practice in such a way that its effects are recognizable in one's daily life over an extended period of time. A response that is internalized pertains to such fundamental matters that it is usually made only after great long-term consideration and is altered only rarely—and then only with much difficulty. Certainly, the fundamental legal consequences of the evangelical counsels professed by religious are—or ought to be—in this category, as well as legal articulations regarding prayer, reconciliation, continuing formation, and the like.

Whether a religious responds by compliance or identification or internalization to various norms depends also on the personality, past experiences, and future perspectives of the one responding. There are often gaps in the conscious and unconscious awareness we have of ourselves, in our cognitive, affective and volitional personal development, and in the perception of our ideal versus real selves. A well-integrated person grows in his or her ability to live a meaningful, joyful, freely chosen, properly motivated life of ongoing change despite these unavoidable gaps. That is, indeed, what is expected of any Christian. It seems that religious, however, often fall prey to an extremist tendency that sometimes all too easily transforms minor matters into ones of major consequence. The placement of a chair, the fold of a napkin or the color of a wall can be—upon occasion—somehow apparently connected to one's eternal salvation and given attention and energy worthy of sublime and eternal matters. In other words, internalization responses can be afforded matters of compliance or of identification, or the reverse can occur. The problem in such situations is primarily that one's gaps are usually being filled with a misplaced legal response with no genuine growth occurring, and the result in such situations is most frequently that the wonderful works of the Lord are buried in monumental trivia with genuine detriment to one another. All religious who have been through the nearly two decades of constitutional revision since Vatican II know how difficult it has been at times to recognize, sort our and articulate the different levels of value and norm for any institute. At the moment in religious renewal, however, the difference between compliance, identification and internalization should be more evident than it was prior to these revisions. The caution for the future is that the once articulated norms do not become inappropriately transferred from one level of response to another by an unreflective and irresponsible approach to law.

Proper interpretation of law can be a helpful tool for a responsible approach to law. This interpretation is accomplished by adverting to elements of the norm(s), the person(s) and the situation(s) at hand. From the perspective of legal norm, it should be noted that any law is the product of history articulated to ensure some value. As such, each norm is a form of communication that should be dealt with in context, as written, with its own level of authority, while being aware of different forms of communication, documentation levels, the evolving meanings of words and various other options. From the perspective of persons, one should be aware of his or her own approach to reality, extent of experience, acceptance of limitations and ability to act prudently with counsel and responsibility. From the perspective of situations or circumstances, an interpreter of the law should always firmly ground the articulations of the code in the initiatives of Vatican II, in the purpose and function of church law, and in the phenomenon of custom as the best real life interpreter. Thus, the second caution of these concluding comments is to know yourself, be properly informed and have genuine concern for those you serve. There simply are no substitutes for self-awareness, solid knowledge and love of the People of God. Nor can any of these be "faked" for long without great harm eventually resulting.

Legal Fallacies

A fallacy is a deception, a false idea, something that causes one to err. A "legal" fallacy is one that causes mistakes to be made regarding law—understanding it, interpreting it or applying it. There are apparently no lists of formal "legal" fallacies, as there are in all elementary philosophy books of "logical" fallacies, so that the interpreter of law can be forewarned—and consequently forearmed—about them. There are, however, some more common "legal" fallacies which we all experience to a greater or lesser degree and which are listed below with fictitious names and descriptions—but whose similarity to actual situations in religious life is definitely more than coincidental.

The Fallacy of Mistaken Identity: This generally confuses theology with law, internals with externals, sacraments with ritual, efficacy with validity, often allowing legal norms to dominate deeper mysteries to the detriment of both.

The Fallacy of Interpreting Intentions: This generally operates to change something someone has actually said into something he or she did not really mean or "Even though you said this, I know what you meant (which was that)." Or—better yet—"Even though you haven't said anything, I know what you're thinking so I don't have to bother to ask."

"It's-Been-Done, So-It's-Possible (and Right)" Fallacy: This is a perfectly valid philosophical principle which becomes a legal fallacy when used by people who want to do something—with or without a sound basis—go ahead and do it and subsequently base the validity and correctness of further action on what was done.

The "What-Hasn't-Been-Done-Isn't-Possible" Fallacy: A subtitle for this fallacy is "And even if you do it and well, it will not be recognized as possible," because those who fall into this one are usually unwilling to learn from reality in the first place and seek to control the world by negative *fiat* refusing to recognize that there may be other reasons why something is not being done than the reason "It is not possible."

The Ecclesiastical-End-Run Fallacy: This fallacy operates in the manner of the backfield of any football team—the designated runner takes the ball and angles around the outside (properly protected by the maneuvers of others) to get to the highest authority first in order to get what he or she wants. It is used not uncommonly in religious life as a fallacy to "angle around" the law or one's own responsibilities or another's rights.

Fallacy of the S.W.A.T. Squad Syndrome: To understand this fallacy one needs at least a vague familiarity with the television program (from which the fallacy takes its name) in which a specially prepared "strategic weapons attack team" routinely engage in such endeavors as calling out several tanks to blow up a building if someone reports a fly on the wall. The parallel in law is use of extreme responses with full legal consequences for minor matters which could (and perhaps ought to) be dealt with in other more constructive ways.

The Isolated-Universalized-Exception Fallacy: This fallacy could be subtitled the "personal power syndrome" because it primarily manifests itself in a person who likes something a certain way or does not like something a certain way and by positive or negative *fiat* decides that this something—pleasing or displeasing to him or her—will henceforth be done or not done by everyone in a particular manner. The results of this fallacy are a plethora of personal preferences imposed as law.

The Legal-Retrojection Fallacy: This historically myopic fallacy perceives the future only in the light of a very recent past (usually about a century or so) which is incorrectly projected backwards to the early centuries and is just as incorrectly considered irrevocably normative for the present.

One could go on and on—depending on imagination and experience—naming and describing legal fallacies. The caution here is two-fold: (1) if religious see themselves at all in the mirror of these mistaken uses of legal norms, perhaps some of them will be avoided; and (2) if the ones we do not manage to avoid are recognized for what they are—mistakes—our responses can perhaps be tempered with a healthy portion of good humor without which life is very dull indeed and sometimes almost unbearable.

A Few Woes

To end these considerations by returning to the beginning (of the book) and to the basis for all Christian reflection (the Word of God), let us note that the legalists of Scripture fare even less well with Jesus than they do with Paul—and rightfully so. The Pharisees and doctors of the law have made it a burden by taking law out of its proper perspective, by distorting its meaning through convenient interpretations, and by looking to law for a power it does not have (Lk 11:42-54). Religious of today—not just the doctors of the law—can be equally astute in straining out the gnats of fulfilling the legal norm while swallowing the camels of compromising the Good News. Whence, the following contemporary "woes" are offered as the final caution for us all:

> **Woe** to the religious who looks to the law hoping it will accomplish what it has no power to do.
> **Woe** to the religious who looks to the law for justification of past, present or future actions.
> **Woe** to the religious who looks to the law for freedom from responsible creativity.
> **Woe** to the religious who looks to the law for an escape from the tensions of real life.
> **Woe** to the religious who looks to the law for ritual purity or guaranteed virtue or human brands of holiness.
> **Woe** to the religious who lets rhetoric outstrip reality or convenience replace commitment or selfishness replace service and looks to the law as a means of explaining away these unfortunate phenomena.
> And **woe** to the religious who abandons or discards the help of law on the pretext of following Christ who himself has completely fulfilled and given true meaning to it.

But **woe** especially and most of all, to the religious who allows anyone or anything to replace the following of Christ to which he or she has been called and is committed, for Christ alone should be—and should be seen to be—the ultimate determining factor of our lives.

Appendix I
Chronology of the Revision Process

January	1959	John XXIII announces Vatican Council II and the revision of the 1917 Code of Canon Law
March	1963	Appointment of the first members of the commission for revision of the code
November	1963	Commission postpones actual revision until after the completion of Vatican Council II
April	1964	Consultors are added to the original commission for revision
November	1965	Decision is made to formulate separate codes for the Latin rite and Oriental rites, as well as a "Fundamental Law" for the entire Church
October	1966	Commission for revision prepares ten principles to guide the revision process
October	1967	First Synod of Bishops approves the Principles for Revision
	1969	Initial publication of *Communicationes,* the official journal of the commission for revision
	1972	Consultation on the *Lex Ecclesiae Fundamentalis* or "Fundamental Law of the Church"
	1972	Consultation on Schema concerning Administrative Procedure
	1973	Consultation on Schema concerning Sanctions

	1975	Consultation on Schema concerning Sacramental Law
	1976	Consultation on Schema concerning Processes
	1977	Consultation on Schema concerning Law for Consecrated Life (Latin/English text published by the U.S.C.C.)
May	1980	Commission for revision judges the revision process completed and circulates the "1980 Schema" combining the results of the consultations on the various separate schemata
October	1980	Synod of Bishops requests an additional "round" of consultation
April	1981	Request for additional consultation is denied and the commission is expanded by John Paul II
October	1981	Final "relatio" (business meeting to make changes) is held at a plenary session of the commission for revision with the final draft (the "1980 Schema" with the changes from the "relatio" incorporated) forwarded to John Paul II
January	1983	Promulgation of the 1983 *Codex Iuris Canonici* to take effect the First Sunday of Advent 1983

APPENDIX II
Principles Guiding the Revision of the Code of Canon Law

The following general principles regarding the process of revision were formulated by the commission for revision in 1966, approved by the first Synod of Bishops in 1967, published in the first edition of *Communicationes* in 1969 and are summarized by Richard G. Cunningham in *The Jurist* 30(1970):447–55.

1. Maintain a basically juridical text with an approach that is pastoral in animation but juridical in form as is required by the social nature and hierarchical structure of the Church.
2. Avoid conflicts wherever possible between matters of conscience and external social matters (known as conflicts between internal and external fora).
3. Legislate in such a way that the juridical norms correspond to the supernatural purpose of the Church and so that charity, temperance, humaneness, and moderation as well as justice and equity are evident. Use instructions, exhortations and recommendations whenever a legal obligation is not strictly necessary.
4. Incorporate in the new code all the post-Vatican II special faculties that have been granted to ordinaries and other superiors so that the office of bishop and his dispensing power are implemented in accord with Vatican II.

5. Incorporate the Vatican II principle of subsidiarity at every level of the people of God so that appropriate particular legislation can implement the healthy, autonomous, executive and legislative power provided for in the general law.
6. Identify the juridical status common to all in the Church originating from each one's human dignity and baptism and which is functionally qualified by the rights and duties of those exercising diverse ecclesiastical ministries but which eliminates the arbitrary use of power as prohibited by divine, natural, and ecclesiastical law.
7. Recognize and protect real and proper subjective rights equally for all persons in the Church eliminating the suspicion of arbitrariness in ecclesiastical administration and providing for administrative recourse in ecclesiastical practice and the administration of justice.
8. Maintain the principle of territoriality as a determinative norm for any portion of the people of God while allowing for other bases of determination as indicated by Vatican II when usefulness to a rite or nation or particular group of persons so indicates.
9. Reduce the number of automatic penalties suppressing all those that appear counterproductive to the purpose of the Church so that penalties in the new code are both few and directed towards the positive ammendment of individuals concerned in matters regarding serious violations.
10. Revise the format of the new code to parallel the *munera* (sanctifying, teaching, ruling) of the Church as indicated in Vatican II so that it deals with (1) legal sources, actions and juridical conditions, (2) the people of God in general and in particular, (3) the three works of the Church (the magisterium, the sacraments, the exercise of power), (4) the temporal goods of the Church and their administration, (5) penal legislation, (6) legislation concerning the juridical and administrative protection of rights.

APPENDIX III
Additional Information on Interim Legislation

[Author's comment: There has been no attempt in the text, nor is there an attempt in this Appendix, to treat exhaustively the plethora of legislation that has been issued concerning religious life in the two decades since Vatican II. Some documents one might expect to find here have been omitted because they are exhortatory (such as *Evangelica testificatio*) or are nonlegislative combinations of former legislation (such as *Mutuae relationes*) or are, in fact, postcodal not strictly legislative documents (such as *Essential Elements*). Only some key documents whose effect can be seen more or less directly in the 1983 code are explained. The documents which were presented chronologically in Chapter 5 are presented here in alphabetical order by *incipit*.]

Cum admotae, pontifical rescript issued by the papal Secretariat of State, November 6, 1964

CA #14 in effect granted the faculty to certain superiors in clerical institutes to dispense the vows of those in temporary profession, and this has been included in c. 688.2. CA #15, which was a major change from the 1917 code (c. 606.2), allowed these superiors to permit absence from the religious house for up to one year under certain restricted circumstances. This has been incorporated in the new c. 665.1. CA ##15 and 17, respectively, permitted those in simple vows to renounce part of their patrimony and to change their last will and testament. Renunciation of patrimony by those in simple vows had been forbidden by the 1917 code, and alteration of one's will required permission of the Apostolic See. Both of these CA changes have been included in the new c. 668. CA #18 concerned transfer of the novitiate house by an act of the competent authority, and this is now part of c. 647.

Ecclesiae sanctae, motu proprio of Paul VI, August 6, 1966.
ES I ##22–40 restricted the meaning of exemption so that it pertained only to the internal matters of any institute. This new meaning along with the corresponding greater authority of the bishop are reflected in the new canons concerning apostolate, especially cc. 674, 678–683. The requirements for an extraordinary general chapter (ES II, ##1, 3, 4, 6), for general participation (ES II, #2), for rewriting constitutions (ES II, #1, 12–14), and for adjustments in prayer life (ES II, #20–22) in common life (ES II, #25–27) and in formation (ES II, #33–38) were all delineated in this interim legislative document. Since ES was the document indicating how to implement the general directives of PC, the content of the latter—rather than the former—is more evident in specific canons of the new code, but the processes of ES are probably more familiar to religious than are the subsequent canons at this point in time.

Pastorale munus, faculties issued *motu proprio* by Paul VI, November 30, 1963.
Among the entries in PM affecting religious, #34 regarding entrance to and exit from the enclosure for nuns has be-

come—with a slight variation—c. 667.4 of the 1983 code. PM #34 was also important because, even after the promulgation of *Venite seorsum* [VS] in 1969, the bishops could continue to exercise this faculty although their powers regarding entrance and exit in VS were somewhat more restrictive. PM #38 regarding transfer between diocesan institutes was a major change from c. 632 of the 1917 code, which required Apostolic See approval for such transfer. PM #38 has been further altered in the new code so that the internal governing authority is competent to act in these matters according to c. 684. PM #39 on the right to dismiss a religious from the diocese for a very serious reason and following certain procedures has become—almost verbatim—the new c. 679.

Perfectae caritatis, decree of Vatican Council II, October 28, 1965.The call of PC #2 to return to the sources of Christian life, to the original inspiration of the institute and to adapt to the current conditions and needs of the church is reflected in cc. 578, 587, 598, 662, 675 and 677. The primacy of the spiritual life mentioned in PC ##5 and 6 appears anew in cc. 573, 607, 608, 619, 630, 652, 661–664 and 673–675. Chastity, poverty and obedience as treated in PC ##12–14 are the foundation of cc. 599–602 as well as 618–619. The common life of PC #15 is reflected in cc. 602, 607–608 and 665. Habit as mentioned in PC #17 has become part of c. 669. The new universal law entries on secular institutes (cc. 710–730) and conferences of major superiors (cc. 708–709) are taken from PC ##11 and 23, respectively. The inclusion of continuing formation in the new code (cc. 659–661) follows from PC #18; that of collective witness to poverty (c. 640), from PC #13; and that of adaptation in the (c. 677), from PC ##8 and 20.

Religionum laicalium, faculties granted by the Sacred Congregation for Religious, May 31, 1966.The major difference between these faculties and those of CA were the persons who could exercise them, with the subject of the powers in RL being certain superiors of lay institutes. Absence from the house (RL #4), renouncing patrimony (RL #5), changing of wills (RL #6) and transfer of the novitiate house (RL #7) were permitted with the same conditions for consent of council as in CA. RL #3, however, required the superiors of lay religious institutes to seek a dispensation of vows for those in temporary profession from the local ordinary. The new code combines elements of CA and RL but does not distinguish between the subject of the powers as being clerical religious or lay religious in cc. 647, 665, 668 and 688.

Renovationis causam, instruction by the Sacred Congregation for Religious and Secular Institutes, January 6, 1969.RC #7 and ##34–36 introduced the notion of promises in preparation for perpetual vows. This notion was eventually dropped by cc. 607 and 654 of the new code, but many institutes in response to RC had introduced promises into their formation program requiring a postcodal clarification by SCRSI (see Appendix IV). RC #13 noted that religious life began with the novitiate, and this was incorporated in c. 646. Options for the place of novitiate as approved by the competent internal authority mentioned in RC ##16–19 have become parts of c. 647. A twelve-month to two-year novitiate with absence up to three months and provision for interspersed apostolic activity as in RL ##21–25 have become—with some alterations—cc. 648–649. RL #37's three year minimum and nine year maximum for temporary profession are basically contained in cc. 655 and 657. The possibility of departure after profession and later re-entry to the same institute without the requirement of repeating the novitiate, a possibility first introduced in RL #38, is contained with slight alteration in c. 690.

APPENDIX IV
Transitional Documents

On February 2, 1984, two decrees, both dated January 31, were issued by the Sacred Congregation for Religious and Secular Institutes. One, beginning with the words *Iuris canonici codice,* concerned steps to be taken regarding constitutions containing prescriptions contrary to the 1983 code. The other, beginning with the words *Prescriptis canonum,* concerned how promises pronounced by members of religious institutes at first commitments made prior to the 1983 code should be treated at the time of renewal or of perpetual profession.

Iuris canonici codice began by noting that some items in already approved constitutions might be contrary to the new code, while other items required by the new code might be missing in the proper law of an institute. Since c. 6.1 of the new code cancels the effects of all contrary legal prescriptions (including those in the proper law of a religious institute), the supreme moderator of each institute acting jointly with the participation of his or her council should explain these matters to the members of the institute. SCRSI authorized the supreme moderator, again acting jointly with his or her council to formulate new norms for the proper law of the institute in order to fill the gaps indicated by the new code or created by the cancellation of contrary laws. Whatever the supreme moderator and council acting jointly might decide would take effect immediately and remain in force until the next regularly scheduled general chapter whose right and duty it is to legislate for the institute. When the chapter acts on the matters concerned, they may be put into practice immediately—provided nothing enacted is contrary to universal law—but such changes in an institute's proper law must still be submitted for approval to the competent authority. For monasteries of nuns the supreme authority of the order or someone specifically delegated by the Holy See will attend to the matters mentioned.

In order to implement this decree:

(1) The supreme moderator—that is, the person in charge of the entire institute (provincials do not qualify)—must act jointly with the council (the technical term used is *collegialiter*) which means that they act as a single unit. Legally speaking, therefore, it is the group acting rather than the supreme moderator acting with the deliberative vote of the council, the action being governed by cc. 140.2 and 119#2.

(2) The group is given the responsibility (a) to identify the matters in the proper law of the institute contrary to or lacking after the 1983 code, (b) to inform the institute's membership in this regard, and (c) to formulate required norms which take effect immediately and hold until the next regularly scheduled general chapter.

Ordinarily, it is the exclusive right of the general chapter to legislate (c. 630), and this faculty actually constitutes temporary legislative power which is an exception to the universal law. As such, according to the canonical rules for interpreting exceptions to the law (c. 18), the power should be interpreted strictly—that is, using it only as truly necessary and within the exact meaning of the words. Thus only matters truly contrary to the code and only relatively important ones—such as, requirements for the validity of novitiate or profession—should be dealt with immediately, leaving whatever can be left to the deliberations of the next regularly scheduled general chapter. Given the extensive responsibilities of general chapters subsequent to Vatican II and the amount of both time and collective effort that have been invested in reformulating the proper law of institutes, it would be in keeping with neither the spirit nor the letter of the law for supreme moderators and councils to seize upon this faculty as an opportunity to enact or reformulate extensive legislation for any institute. Only what is truly necessary and truly contrary should be addressed with the faculty granted in this decree, and these in such a way that the norms of universal law are fulfilled with the spirit of the institute's previous revisions being kept constantly in mind.

(3) The next regularly scheduled general chapter must deliberate concerning the matters of the proper law contrary to or missing according to the new code and incorporate appropriate new norms into the proper law. That is, the chapter must address all those items enacted by the supreme moderator and council as well as any other matters that are not certainly contrary or are of less importance and, thus, may not have been reformulated in accord with the faculty granted in this decree. The new norms of the general chapter must then be approved by the competent authority (diocesan bishop for diocesan institutes and SCRSI for pontifical institutes), but they take effect when enacted by the chapter and before this required approbation is received provided such new norms are not also contrary to the code.

(4) For monasteries of nuns the faculty granted by this decree belongs to the supreme authority of the order—not to the supreme moderator and council acting jointly—or to a special delegate of the Holy See. Who constitutes the supreme authority of the order for any monastery of nuns can be accurately determined by checking the government section of their own constitutions and may, in fact, differ from group to group. A special delegate of the Holy See will probably be appointed in cases such as federations which have no one supreme authority who has extensive power over the member monasteries. Thus

it appears that temporary decisions regarding their lives—which are allowed for every other institute of consecrated life and of which nuns ought to be capable—are for some reason not permitted to cloistered contemplative women.

Prescriptis canonum, a very short decree, stated that by cc. 607.2, 653.2 and 654 of the new code promises no longer constitute a form of profession in a religious institute. From now on those novices being incorporated must profess public vows, and those who may have previously made promises must profess public vows at the time of renewal of profession or of perpetual profession. For this latter group the time in promises may be included in the three years of temporary vows required for the validity of perpetual vows.

In order to implement this decree:

(1) Only those institutes in which promises have been introduced and in which some novices have actually made commitment by promises and are still bound by such promises need be concerned.

(2) Persons who are in promises need not immediately pronounce temporary or perpetual vows but should do so according to whatever is next in progression for the required processes of continuing formation after initial incorporation (i.e., the next chronological step after initial promises). Some persons may perchance have made commitment by promises "until the time of profession by vows" or "until the time of perpetual profession"—a practice not legally advisable but recently done in some institutes. The decree does not address this situation, but—using the canonical rules for dealing with gaps in the law—it would seem that those who have been in such promises for three years or more and are ready to make perpetual profession should do so by public vow at an appropriate time in the near future. Those who have not yet been committed for three years or who, although committed for three

years or more, are not ready to make perpetual profession may wish to pronounce public temporary vows for a specific time period at some opportune occasion in the near future, but this is not required by the decree.

(3) Any previous period of commitment by promises made according to the proper law of the institute is to be counted and suffices for the three years of temporary profession by public vow specified in c. 655 and required for validity of perpetual profession in c. 658#2 of the 1983 code. Thus any person who has been committed by promises need not, and indeed should not, immediately make temporary profession and begin counting the required three years again.

APPENDIX V
Canons of the 1983 Code Concerning Institutes of Consecrated Life Canons 573–709

Taken from *Code of Canon Law, Latin-English Edition*, copyright 1983 by the Canon Law Society of America, reprinted with permission.

BOOK II
THE PEOPLE OF GOD

PART III
INSTITUTES OF CONSECRATED LIFE
AND SOCIETIES OF APOSTOLIC LIFE

SECTION I
INSTITUTES OF CONSECRATED LIFE

TITLE I
NORMS COMMON TO ALL INSTITUTES
OF CONSECRATED LIFE

Can. 573 — §1. Life consecrated by the profession of the evangelical counsels is a stable form of living by which faithful, following Christ more closely under the action of the Holy Spirit, are totally dedicated to God who is loved most of all, so that, having dedicated themselves to His honor, the upbuilding of the Church and the salvation of the world by a new and special title, they strive for the perfection of charity in service to the Kingdom of God and, having become an outstanding sign in the Church, they may foretell the heavenly glory.

§2. Christian faithful who profess the evangelical counsels of chastity, poverty and obedience by vows or other sacred bonds according to the proper laws of institutes freely assume this form of living in institutes of consecrated life canonically erected by competent church authority and through the charity to which these counsels lead they are joined to the Church and its mystery in a special way.

Can. 574 — §1. The state of those who profess the evangelical counsels in institutes of this kind pertains to the life and sanctity of the Church and for this reason is to be fostered and promoted by all in the Church.

§2. Certain Christian faithful are specially called to this state by God so that they may enjoy a special gift in the life of the Church and contribute to its salvific mission according to the purpose and spirit of the institute.

Can. 575 — The evangelical counsels, based on the teaching and examples of Christ the Teacher, are a divine gift which the Church has received from the Lord and always preserves through His grace.

Can. 576 — It belongs to the competent authority of the Church to interpret the evangelical counsels, to regulate their practice by laws, to constitute therefrom stable forms of living by canonical approbation, and, for its part, to take care that the institutes grow and flourish according to the spirit of the founders and wholesome traditions.

Can. 577 — In the Church there are very many institutes of consecrated life which have different gifts according to the grace which has been given them: they follow Christ more closely as He prays, announces the Kingdom of God, performs good works for people, shares His life with them in the world, and yet always does the will of the Father.

Can. 578 — The intention of the founders and their determination concerning the nature, purpose, spirit and character of the institute which have been ratified by competent ecclesiastical authority as well as its wholesome traditions, all of which constitute the patrimony of the institute itself, are to be observed faithfully by all.

Can. 579 — Diocesan bishops each in his own territory can erect institutes of consecrated life by a formal decree, provided that the Apostolic See has been consulted.

Can 580 — The aggregation of one institute of consecrated life to another is reserved to the competent authority of the aggregating institute, always safeguarding the canonical autonomy of the aggregated institute.

Can. 581 — Dividing an institute into parts, whatever the parts are called, erecting new ones, joining previously erected parts or defining them in another way pertains to the competent authority of the institute, in accord with the norm of the constitutions.

Can. 582 — Mergers and unions of institutes of consecrated life are reserved to the Apostolic See alone; confederations and federations are also reserved to it.

Can. 583 — Changes in institutes of consecrated life which affect matters which have been approved by the Apostolic See cannot be made without its permission.

Can. 584 — Suppressing an institute pertains to the Apostolic See alone, to whom also it is reserved to determine what is to be done with the temporal goods of the institute.

Can. 585 — Suppressing parts of an institute pertains to the competent authority of the institute itself.

Can. 586 — §1. For individual institutes there is acknowledged a rightful autonomy of life, especially of governance, by which they enjoy their own discipline in the Church and have the power to preserve their own patrimony intact as mentioned in can. 578.

§2. It belongs to local ordinaries to safeguard and protect this autonomy.

Can. 587 — §1. In order to protect more faithfully the particular vocation and identity of each institute, its fundamental code or constitutions must contain, besides what must be observed according to can. 578, fundamental norms about the governance of the institute and the discipline of members, the incorporation and formation of members, and the proper object of sacred bonds.

§2. A code of this kind is approved by the competent authority of the church and can be changed only with its consent.

§3. In this code spiritual and juridical elements are to be suitably joined together; however norms are not to be multiplied unless it is necessary.

§4. Other norms established by the competent authority of the institute are to be suitably collected in other codes, which can moreover be fittingly reviewed and adapted according to the needs of places and times.

Appendix V

Can. 588 — §1. The state of consecrated life by its very nature is neither clerical nor lay.

§2. An institute is said to be clerical if, by reason of the purpose or design intended by its founder or in virtue of legitimate tradition, it is under the supervision of clerics, it assumes the exercise of sacred orders, and it is recognized as such by church authority.

§3. An institute is called lay if recognized as such by church authority, by virtue of its nature, character and purpose it has a proper function defined by the founder or by legitimate tradition which does not include the exercise of sacred orders.

Can. 589 — An institute of consecrated life is said to be of pontifical right if it has been erected by the Apostolic See or approved by a formal decree of the Apostolic See; on the other hand an institute is said to be of diocesan right if, after having been erected by a diocesan bishop, it has not obtained a decree of approval from the Apostolic See.

Can 590 — §1. Institutes of consecrated life, inasmuch as they are dedicated in a special way to the service of God and of the entire Church, are subject to the supreme authority of this same Church in a special manner.

§2. Individual members are also bound to obey the Supreme Pontiff as their highest superior by reason of the sacred bond of obedience.

Can. 591 — In order to provide better for the good of institutes and the needs of the apostolate, the Supreme Pontiff, by reason of his primacy over the universal Church and considering the common good, can exempt institutes of consecrated life from the governance of local ordinaries and subject them either to himself alone or to another ecclesiastical authority.

Can. 592 — §1. In order that the communion of institutes with the Apostolic See be better fostered each supreme moderator is to send a brief report on the status and life of the institute to the Apostolic See in a manner and at a time determined by the latter.

§2. The moderators of every institute are to promote knowledge of the documents of the Holy See which affect members entrusted to them and be concerned about their observance of them.

Can. 593 — With due regard for the prescription of can. 586, institutes of pontifical right are immediately and exclusively subject to the power of the Apostolic See in internal governance and discipline.

Can. 594 — With due regard for can. 586, an institute of diocesan right remains under the special care of the diocesan bishop.

Can. 595 — §1. It belongs to the bishop of the principal seat of the institute to approve the constitutions and confirm any changes legitimately introduced into them, except in those matters in which the Apostolic See has intervened; it also belongs to him to deal with business of greater importance which affects the whole institute and which are beyond the power of its internal authority; he does so after consulting other diocesan bishops if the institute has spread to several dioceses.

§2. The diocesan bishop can grant dispensations from the constitutions in particular cases.

Can. 596 — §1. Superiors and chapters of institutes enjoy that power over members which is defined in universal law and the constitutions.

§2. Moreover, in clerical religious institutes of pontifical right they also possess ecclesiastical power of governance for both the external and the internal forum.

§3. The prescriptions of cann. 131, 133 and 137–144 are applicable to the power referred to in §1.

Can. 597 — §1. Any Catholic, endowed with a right intention, who has the qualities required by universal and proper law and who is not prevented by any impediment can be admitted to an institute of consecrated life.

§2. No one can be admitted without suitable preparation.

Can. 598 — §1. Each institute, keeping in mind its own character and purposes is to define in its constitutions the manner in which the evangelical counsels of chastity, poverty and obedience are to be observed for its way of living.

§2. All members must not only observe the evangelical counsels faithfully and fully, but also organize their life according to the proper law of the institute and thereby strive for the perfection of their state.

Can. 599 — The evangelical counsel of chastity assumed for the sake of the kingdom of heaven, as a sign of the future world and a source of more abundant fruitfulness in an undivided heart, entails the obligation of perfect continence in celibacy.

Can. 600 — The evangelical counsel of poverty in imitation of Christ who, although He was rich became poor for us, entails, besides a life which is poor in fact and in spirit, a life of labor lived in moderation and foreign to earthly riches, a dependence and a limitation in the use and disposition of goods according to the norm of the proper law of each institute.

Can. 601 — The evangelical counsel of obedience, undertaken in a spirit of faith and love in the following of Christ who was obedient even unto death requires a submission of the will to legitimate superiors, who stand in the place of God when they command according to the proper constitutions.

Can. 602 — The life of brothers or sisters proper to each institute, by which all members are united together like a special family in Christ, is to be determined in such a way that it becomes a mutual support for all in fulfilling the vocation of each member. Moreover by their communion as brothers or sisters, rooted in and built on love, the members are to be an example of universal reconciliation in Christ.

Can. 603 — §1. Besides institutes of consecrated life, the Church recognizes the eremitic or anchoritic life by which the Christian faithful devote their life to the praise of God and salvation of the world through a stricter separation from the world, the silence of solitude and assiduous prayer and penance.

§2. A hermit is recognized in the law as one dedicated to God in a consecrated life if he or she publicly professes the three evangelical counsels, confirmed by a vow or other sacred bond, in the hands of the diocesan bishop and observes his or her own plan of life under his direction.

Can. 604 — §1. Similar to these forms of consecrated life is the order of virgins, who, committed to the holy plan of following Christ more closely, are consecrated to God by the diocesan bishop according to the approved liturgical rite, are betrothed mystically to Christ, the Son of God, and are dedicated to the service of the Church.

§2. In order to observe their commitment more faithfully and to perform by mutual support service to the Church which is in harmony with their state these virgins can form themselves into associations.

Can. 605 — Approving new forms of consecrated life is reserved to the Apostolic See alone. Diocesan bishops, however, should strive to discern new gifts of consecrated life granted to the Church by the Holy Spirit and they should aid their promoters so that they can express their proposals as well as possible and protect them with suitable statutes, utilizing especially the general norms contained in this section.

Can. 606 —Whatever is determined about institutes of consecrated life and their members applies equally to either sex, unless the contrary is apparent from the context of the wording or nature of the matter.

TITLE II
RELIGIOUS INSTITUTES

Can. 607 — §1. Religious life, as a consecration of the whole person, manifests in the Church a wonderful marriage brought about by God, a sign of the future age. Thus religious bring to perfection their full gift as a sacrifice offered to God by which their whole existence becomes a continuous worship of God in love.

§2. A religious institute is a society in which members, according to proper law, pronounce public vows either perpetual or temporary, which are to be renewed when they have lapsed, and live a life in common as brothers or sisters.

§3. The public witness to be rendered by religious to Christ and to the Church entails a separation from the world proper to the character and purpose of each institute.

CHAPTER I
RELIGIOUS HOUSES AND THEIR ERECTION AND SUPPRESSION

Can. 608 — A religious community must live in a house legitimately constituted under the authority of the superior designated according to the norm of law; each house is to have at least an oratory in which the Eucharist is celebrated and reserved so that it truly is the center of the community.

Can. 609 — §1. Houses of a religious institute are erected by the competent authority according to the constitutions with the previous written consent of the diocesan bishop.

§2. In order to erect a monastery of nuns the permission of the Apostolic See is also required.

Can. 610 — §1. The erection of houses takes place with due regard for their usefulness for the Church and the institute and safeguarding those things which are required for the correct living out of the religious life of the members according to the specific purposes and spirit of the institute.

§2. No house is to be erected unless it can be prudently judged that the needs of the members will be suitably provided for.

Can. 611 — The consent of the diocesan bishop to erect a religious house of any institute brings with it the right:

1° to lead a life according to its own character and the purposes of the institute;

2° to exercise the works proper to the institute according to the norm of law, with due regard for any conditions attached to the consent;

3° for clerical institutes to have a church, with due regard for the prescription of can. 1215, §3, and to perform sacred ministries, observing what is by law to be observed.

Can. 612 — In order that a religious house be converted to apostolic works different from those for which it was established the consent of the diocesan bishop is required; but this is not so if it is a matter of a change which refers only to internal government and discipline, with due regard for the laws of the foundation.

Can. 613 — §1. A religious house of canons regular and monks under the governance and care of its own moderator is autonomous unless the constitutions state otherwise.

§2. A moderator of an autonomous house is by law a major superior.

Can. 614 — Monasteries of nuns which are associated with an institute of men maintain their own order of life and governance according to the constitutions. Mutual rights and obligations are to be so defined that the association is spiritually enriching.

Can. 615 — An autonomous monastery which has no other major superior beyond its own moderator and is not associated with any other institute of religious in such a way that the superior of the latter enjoys true power over such a monastery determined by the constitutions is committed to the special vigilance of the diocesan bishop according to the norm of law.

Can. 616 — §1. A legitimately erected religious house can be suppressed by the supreme moderator according to the norm of the constitutions after having consulted the diocesan bishop. The proper law of the institute is to provide for the goods of the suppressed house, with due regard for the wills of the founders and donors or for legitimately acquired rights.

§2. The suppression of the only house of an institute pertains to the Holy See, to which is also reserved the right to determine what is to be done in that case with its goods.

§3. The suppression of an autonomous house, such as that described in can. 613, belongs to the general chapter, unless the constitutions state otherwise.

§4. The suppression of an autonomous monastery of nuns pretains to the Apostolic see, with due regard for the prescriptions of the constitutions with regard to its goods.

Chapter II
THE GOVERNANCE OF INSTITUTES

Art. 1
Superiors and Councils

Can. 617 — Superiors are to fulfill their duty and exercise their power according to the norm of universal and proper law.

Can. 618 — Superiors are to exercise their power, received from God through the ministry of the Church, in a spirit of service. Therefore, docile to the will of God in carrying out their duty, they are to govern their subjects as children of God and, promoting their voluntary obedience with reverence for the human person, they are to listen to them willingly and foster their working together for the good of the institute and of the Church, but with the superiors' authority to decide and prescribe what must be done remaining intact.

Can. 619 — Superiors are to devote themselves to their office assiduously and, together with the members entrusted to them, they should be eager to build a community of brothers or sisters in Christ in which God is sought after and loved before all else. Therefore, they are to nourish the members frequently with the food of the word of God and lead them to the celebration of the sacred liturgy. They are to be an example to the members in cultivating virtues and in the observance of the laws and traditions of the particular institute; they are to meet the personal needs of the members in an appropriate fashion, look after solicitously and visit the sick, admonish the restless, console the faint of heart, and be patient toward all.

Can. 620 — Major superiors are those who govern a whole institute, a province of an institute, some part equivalent to a province, or an autonomous house, as well as their vicars.

Comparable to these are the abbot primate and superior of a monastic congregation, who nonetheless do not have all the power which universal law grants major superiors.

Can. 621 — The grouping of several houses under the same superior which constitutes an immediate part of the institute and which has been canonically erected by the legitimate authority is called a province.

Can. 622 — The supreme moderator holds power over all provinces, houses and members of the institute, which is to be exercised according to proper law; other superiors enjoy power within the limits of their office.

Can. 623 — In order that members be validly appointed or elected to the office of superior, a suitable time is required after perpetual or definitive profession, to be determined by proper law, or if it is a question of major superiors, by the constitutions.

Can. 624 — §1. Superiors are to be constituted for a certain and appropriate amount of time according to the nature and needs of the institute, unless the constitutions state otherwise for the supreme moderator and for superiors of autonomous houses.

§2. Proper law is to provide in suitable norms that superiors constituted for a definite time do not remain too long in offices of governance without an interruption.

§3. Nevertheless they can be removed from office during their term or transferred to another office for reasons determined in proper law.

Can. 625 — §1. The supreme moderator of an institute is to be designated by canonical election according to the norm of the constitutions.

§2. The bishop of the principal seat presides at elections of the superior of an autonomous monastery, mentioned in can. 615, and of the supreme moderator of an institute of diocesan right.

§3. Other superiors are to be constituted according to the norm of the constitutions, but in such a way that if they are elected they need the confirmation of the competent major superior; if they are appointed by the superior, a suitable consultation is to precede.

Can. 626 — Superiors in the conferral of offices and members in elections are to observe the norms of universal and proper law, abstain from any abuse or partiality and name or elect those whom they know in the Lord to be truly worthy and suitable having nothing in mind but God and the good of the institute. Moreover, in elections they are to avoid any procurement of votes either directly or indirectly for themselves or for others.

Can. 627 — §1. According to the norm of the constitutions, superiors are to have their own council, whose assistance they are to use in carrying out their office.

§2. Besides the cases prescribed in universal law, proper law is to determine cases in which consent or counsel is required in order to act validly, which must be obtained in accord with the norm of can. 127.

Can. 628 — §1. Superiors who are designated for this function by the proper law of the institute are to visit the houses and members entrusted to them at the times designated by the norms of this same proper law.

§2. It is the right and the duty of the diocesan bishop to visit even with respect to religious discipline:

1° autonomous monasteries mentioned in can. 615;

2° individual houses of an institute of diocesan right situated in his territory.

§3. Members are to deal in a trusting manner with a visitor, whose legitimate questions they are obliged to answer according to truth in love; moreover no one is permitted in any way to divert members from this obligation or otherwise to impede the scope of the visitation.

Can. 629 — All superiors are to reside in their respective houses and not absent themselves from it, unless according to the norm of proper law.

Can. 630 — §1. Superiors are to recognize the due freedom of their members concerning the sacrament of penance and the direction of conscience, with due regard however for the discipline of the institute.

§2. According to the norm of proper law superiors are to be solicitous that suitable confessors to whom they can confess frequently be available to members.

§3. In monasteries of nuns, in houses of formation and in more numerous lay communities there are to be ordinary confessors approved by the local ordinary after consultation with the community; members nevertheless have no obligation to approach them.

§4. Superiors are not to hear the confessions of their subjects unless the latter request it of their own initiative.

§5. Members are to approach superiors with trust, to whom they can express their minds freely and willingly. However, superiors are forbidden to induce their subjects in any way whatever to make a manifestation of conscience to them.

Art. 2
Chapters

Can. 631 — §1. The general chapter, which holds supreme authority in the institute according to the norm of the constitutions, is to be so formed that, representing the entire institute, it should be a true sign of its unity in love. Its foremost duty is this: to protect the patrimony of the institute mentioned in can. 578, and promote suitable renewal in accord with this patrimony, to elect the supreme moderator, to treat major business matters and to publish norms which all are bound to obey.

§2. The composition and the extent of the power of the chapter is to be defined in the constitutions; proper law is to determine further the order to be observed in the celebration of the chapter, especially regarding elections and procedures for handling various matters.

§3. According to norms determined in proper law, not only provinces and local communities but also any member at all can freely send his or her wishes and suggestions to the general chapter.

Can. 632 — Proper law is to determine clearly what pertains to other chapters of the institute and other similar gatherings, namely, regarding their nature, authority, composition, mode of procedure and time of celebration.

Can. 633 — §1. Organs of participation or consultation are to carry out faithfully the duty entrusted to them according to the norm of universal and proper law and to express in their own way the concern and participation of all members for the good of the entire institute or community.

§2. Wise discretion is to be used in establishing and using these means of participation and consultation, and their procedures are to conform to the character and purpose of the institute.

Art. 3
Temporal Goods and their Administration

Can. 634 — §1. Institutes, provinces and houses, insofar as they are juridic persons by the law itself, are capable of acquiring, possessing, administering and alienating temporal goods, unless this capacity has been excluded or restricted in the constitutions.

§2. Nevertheless, they are to avoid all appearance of luxury, immoderate wealth and amassing of goods.

Can. 635 — §1. The temporal goods of religious institutes, since they are ecclesiastical goods, are regulated by the prescriptions of Book V, *The Temporal Goods of the Church,* unless it is expressly stated otherwise.

§2. Nevertheless, each institute is to determine appropriate norms for the use and administration of goods so that the poverty appropriate to the institute is fostered, protected and expressed.

Can. 636 — §1. In each institute and likewise in each province which is governed by a major superior there is to be a finance officer, distinct from the major superior and constituted according to the norm of proper law, who carries out the administration of goods under the direction of the respective superior. Even in local communities there is to be a finance officer distinct from the local superior to the extent that it is possible.

§2. At the time and in the manner determined by proper law finance officers and other administrators are to render an account of their administrative actions to the competent authority.

Can. 637 — Autonomous monasteries mentioned in can. 615 must render an account of their administration once a year to the local ordinary; moreover, the local ordinary has the right to know about the financial reports of religious houses of diocesan right.

Can. 638 — §1. It is for proper law, within the scope of universal law, to determine acts which exceed the limit and manner of ordinary administration and to determine those things which are necessary to place an act of extraordinary administration validly.

§2. Besides superiors, officials who are designated for this purpose in the proper law can validly incur expenses and perform juridic acts of ordinary administration within the limits of their office.

§3. For the validity of alienation and any other business transaction in which the patrimonial condition of a juridic person can be affected adversely, there is required the written permission of the competent superior with the consent of the council. If, moreover, it concerns a business transaction which exceeds the highest amount defined for a given region by the Holy See, or items given to the Church in virtue of a vow, or items of precious art or of historical value, the permission of the Holy See is also required.

§4. For the autonomous monasteries mentioned in can. 615 and for institutes of diocesan right it is additionally necessary to have the written consent of the local ordinary.

Can. 639 — §1. A juridic person which has contracted debts and obligations even with the permission of the superior is bound to answer for them.

§2. If a member with permission of the superior has made a contract concerning personal goods, the member must answer for it, but if the business of the institute was conducted by order of the superior, the institute must answer.

§3. A religious who has made a contract without any permission of superiors must answer for it, but not the juridic person.

§4. It shall be a fixed rule, nevertheless, that an action can always be brought against one who has profited from the contract entered into.

§5. Religious superiors are to be careful that they do not permit debts to be contracted unless it is certain that the interest on the debt can be paid from ordinary income and that the capital sum can be paid off through legitimate amortization within a time that is not excessively long.

Can. 640 — Taking into account local conditions institutes are to strive to give, as it were, collective witness of charity and poverty and are to contribute what they can of their own goods for the needs of the Church and the sustenance of the poor.

CHAPTER III
ADMISSION OF CANDIDATES AND FORMATION OF MEMBERS

Art. 1
ADMISSION TO THE NOVITIATE

Can. 641 — The right of admitting candidates to the novitiate pertains to major superiors according to the norm of proper law.

Can. 642 — Superiors are to be vigilant about admitting only those who, besides the required age, have health, suitable character and sufficient qualities of maturity to embrace the particular life of the institute; this health, character, and maturity are to be attested to, if necessary by using experts, with due regard for the prescription of can. 220.

Can. 643 — §1. One is invalidly admitted to the novitiate:
  1° who has not yet completed the seventeenth year of age;
  2° who is a spouse, during a marriage;
  3° who is presently held by a sacred bond with any institute of consecrated life or who is incorporated in any society of apostolic life, with due regard for the prescription of can. 684;

4° who enters the institute as a result of force, grave fear or fraud, or whom the superior receives induced in the same way;

5° who has concealed his or her incorporation in any institute of consecrated life or society of apostolic life.

§2. Proper law can establish other impediments to admission, even for validity, or can add other conditions.

Can. 644 — Superiors are not to admit to the novitiate secular clerics if their local ordinary has not been consulted or those who, burdened by debts, cannot repay them.

Can. 645 — §1. Before they are admitted to the novitiate, candidates must show proof of baptism, confirmation and free status.

§2. If it is a question of admitting clerics or those who have been admitted to another institute of consecrated life, a society of apostolic life or a seminary, there is further required the testimony of the local ordinary or major superior of the institute or society or of the rector of the seminary respectively.

§3. Proper law can demand other testimonies about the requisite suitability of candidates and their freedom from impediments.

§4. If it appears necessary superiors can ask for other information, even with the obligation of secrecy.

Art. 2

The Novitiate and Formation of Novices

Can. 646 — The novitiate, by which life in the institute begins, is ordered to this, that the novices better recognize their divine vocation and one which is, moreover, proper to the institute, that they experience the institute's manner of living, that they be formed in mind and heart by its spirit, and that their intention and suitability be tested.

Can. 647 — §1. The erection, transfer and suppression of a novitiate house are to take place through a written decree of the supreme moderator of the institute with the consent of his or her council.

§2. In order to be valid a novitiate must be made in a house properly designated for this purpose. In particular cases and as an exception, by concession of the supreme moderator with the consent of the council, a candidate can make the novitiate in another house of the institute under the guidance of an approved religious who assumes the role of director of novices.

§3. A major superior can permit a group of novices to live for a stated period of time in another house of the institute, designated by the same superior.

Can. 648 — §1. In order that the novitiate be valid it must include twelve months spent in the community of the novitiate itself, with due regard for the prescription of can. 647, §3.

§2. To complete the formation of the novices, in addition to the time mentioned in §1, the constitutions can determine one or several periods of apostolic exercises to be spent outside the novitiate community.

§3. The novitiate is not to extend beyond two years.

Can. 649 — §1. With due regard for the prescriptions of cann. 647, §3, and 648, §2, absence from the novitiate house which lasts more than three months, either continuous or interrupted, renders the novitiate invalid. An absence of more than fifteen days must be made up.

§2. With the permission of the competent major superior first profession can be anticipated, but not by more than fifteen days.

Can. 650 — §1. The scope of the novitiate demands that the novices be formed under the guidance of a director according to the program of training to be defined by the proper law.

§2. The governance of novices is reserved to one director under the authority of the major superiors.

Can. 651 — §1. The director of novices is to be a member of the institute who has professed perpetual vows and is legitimately designated.

§2. If there is a need, assistants can be given to the director to whom they are subject regarding the governance of the novitiate and the program of training.

§3. Members who have been carefully prepared and who, not impeded by other duties, can carry out this duty fruitfully and in a stable manner are to be in charge of the training of novices.

Can. 652 — §1. It is for the director and assistants to discern and test the vocation of the novices and to form them gradually to lead correctly the life of perfection proper to the institute.

§2. The novices are to be led to cultivate human and Christian virtues; they are to be introduced to a fuller way of perfection by prayer and self-denial; they are to be instructed to contemplate the mystery of salvation and to read and meditate on the Sacred Scriptures; they are to be prepared to cultivate the worship of God in the sacred liturgy; they are to be trained in a way of life consecrated by the evangelical counsels to God and humankind in Christ; they are to be educated about the character and spirit, purpose and discipline, history and life of their institute; and they are to be imbued with a love for the Church and its sacred pastors.

§3. Conscious of their own responsibility, the novices are to collaborate actively with their director so that they may faithfully respond to the grace of a divine vocation.

§4. Members of the institute are to take care that on their part they cooperate in the work of training novices by the example of their life and by prayer.

§5. The time of novitiate mentioned in can. 648, §1, is to be employed properly in the work of formation and therefore the novices are not to be occupied with studies and duties which do not directly serve this formation.

Can. 653 — §1. A novice can freely leave an institute; moreover the competent authority of the institute can dismiss a novice.

§2. When the novitiate is completed, a novice, if judged suitable, is to be admitted to temporary profession; otherwise the novice is to be dismissed. If there is a doubt about the novice's suitability, the time of probation can be extended by the major superior according to the norm of proper law, but not more than six months

Art. 3
Religious Profession

Can. 654 — By religious profession members assume by public vow the observance of the three evangelical counsels, are consecrated to God through the ministry of the Church, and are incorporated into the institute with rights and duties defined by law.

Can. 655 — Temporary profession is made for the time defined in proper law, which may not be less than three years and no longer than six.

Can. 656 — For the validity of temporary profession, it is required that:

1° the person who is about to make the profession shall have completed at least the eighteenth year of age;

2° the novitiate has been validly completed;

3° admission has been freely given by the competent superior with the vote of the council in accord with the norm of law;

4° the profession be expressed and made without force, grave fear or fraud;

5° the profession be received by the legitimate superior personally or through another.

Can. 657 — §1. When the time for which the profession has been made has elapsed the religious who freely requests it and is judged suitable is to be admitted to a renewal of profession or to perpetual profession; otherwise the religious is to leave.

§2. If it seems opportune the period of temporary profession can be extended by the competent superior, according to proper law, but in such a way that the entire time in which the member is bound by temporary vows does not exceed nine years.

§3. Perpetual profession can be anticipated for a just cause, but not by more than three months

Can. 658 — Besides the conditions mentioned in can. 656,.3°, 4° and 5° and others attached by proper law, for the validity of perpetual profession the following are required:

1° the completion of at least the twenty-first year of age;

2° previous temporary profession for at least three years, with due regard for the prescription of can. 657, §3.

Art. 4
The Formation of Religious

Can. 659 — §1. In individual institutes after first profession the formation of all members is to be continued so that they may lead more fully the proper life of the institute and carry out its mission more suitably.

§2. Therefore, proper law must define the program of this formation and its duration, keeping in mind the needs of the Church and the circumstances of human persons and times to the extent this is required by the purpose and character of the institute.

§3. The formation of members who are preparing to receive holy orders is regulated by universal law and by the program of studies proper to the institute.

Can. 660 — §1. The formation is to be systematic, adapted to the capacity of the members, spiritual and apostolic, doctrinal and at the same time practical, and when it seems opportune, leading to appropriate degrees both ecclesiastical and civil.

§2. During the time of this formation duties and jobs which would impede the formation are not to be assigned to members.

Can. 661 — Throughout their entire life religious are to continue carefully their own spiritual, doctrinal, and practical formation, and superiors are to provide them with the resources and time to do this.

Chapter iv
THE OBLIGATIONS AND RIGHTS OF INSTITUTES AND THEIR MEMBERS

Can. 662 — Religious are to have as their highest rule of life the following of Christ as proposed in the gospel and expressed in the constitutions of their institute.

Can. 663 — §1. Contemplation of divine things and assiduous union with God in prayer is to be the first and foremost duty of all religious.

§2. Members are to participate in the Eucharistic Sacrifice daily if possible, receive the Most Sacred Body of Christ and adore this same Lord present in the Sacrament.

§3. They should apply themselves to the reading of Sacred Scripture and to mental prayer; they are to celebrate the liturgy of the hours worthily according to the prescriptions of proper law, with due regard for the obligation of clerics in can. 276, §2, 3°, and they are to perform other exercises of piety.

§4. They are to cultivate a special devotion to the Virgin Mother of God, model and protector of all consecrated life, including the Marian rosary.

§5. They are faithfully to observe an annual period of spiritual retreat.

Can. 664 — Religious are to apply themselves to conversion of heart to God, examine their conscience even daily, and frequently approach the sacrament of penance.

Can. 665 — §1. Observing a common life, religious are to live in their own religious house and not be absent from it without the permission of their superior. However, if it is a question of a lengthy absence from the house the major superior for a just cause and with the consent of the council can permit the member to live outside a house of the institute, but not for more than a year, except for the purpose of caring for poor health, for the purpose of studies or of undertaking an apostolate in the name of the institute.

§2. Members unlawfully absent from the religious house with the intention of withdrawing from the power of their superiors are to be solicitously sought after by them and aided to return and persevere in their vocation.

Can. 666 — Necessary discretion is to be observed in the use of media of communication, and whatever is harmful to one's vocation and dangerous to the chastity of a consecrated person is to be avoided.

Can. 667 — §1. In all houses cloister adapted to the character and mission of the institute is to be observed according to the determinations of proper law, with some part of the religious house always being reserved to the members alone.

§2. A stricter discipline of cloister is to be observed in monasteries ordered to the contemplative life.

§3. Monasteries of nuns which are totally ordered to the contemplative life must observe *papal* cloister, namely according to norms given by the Apostolic See. Other monasteries of nuns are to observe cloister adapted to their own character and defined in the constitutions.

§4. For a just cause the diocesan bishop has the faculty of entering the cloister of monasteries of nuns which are in his diocese, and, for a grave cause and with the consent of the superior, of permitting others to enter the cloister and nuns to leave the cloister for a truly necessary period of time.

Can. 668 — §1. Members are to cede the administration of their goods to whomever they prefer before first profession, and unless the constitutions state otherwise, they are freely to make disposition for their use and their revenues. Moreover, they are to draw up a will, which is also valid in civil law, at least before perpetual profession.

§2. In order to change these dispositions for a just cause and to place any act whatsoever in matters of temporal goods they need the permission of the superior who is competent according to the norm of proper law.

§3. Whatever a religious acquires through personal work or by reason of the institute is acquired for the institute. Unless it is otherwise stated in proper law those things which accrue to a religious by way of pension, subsidy or insurance in any way whatever are acquired for the institute.

§4. Those who must renounce their goods completely because of the nature of the institute are to make a renunciation before perpetual profession in a form which, if possible, is also valid in civil law and takes effect from the day of profession. Religious in perpetual vows who wish to renounce their goods either in part or totally according to the norm of proper law and with permission of the supreme moderator are to do the same thing.

§5. Professed religious who have fully renounced all their goods because of the nature of the institute lose the capacity of acquiring and possessing, and therefore invalidly place acts contrary to the vow of poverty. Moreover, those things which accrue to them after the act of renunciation belong to the institute, according to the norm of proper law.

Can. 669 — §1. Religious are to wear the habit of the institute made according to the norm of proper law as a sign of their consecration and as a testimony of poverty.

§2. Clerical religious of an institute which does not have its own habit are to wear clerical dress according to the norm of can. 284.

Can. 670 — An institute must furnish for its members all those things which are necessary according to the norm of the constitutions for achieving the purpose of their vocation.

Can. 671 — A religious is not to accept duties and offices outside the institute without the permission of the legitimate superior.

Can. 672 — Religious are bound by the prescriptions of cann. 277, 285, 286, 287, and 289, and, moreover, religious clerics are bound by the prescriptions of can. 279, §2; in lay institutes of pontifical right, the permission mentioned in can. 285, §4 can be granted by the proper major superior.

Chapter v
THE APOSTOLATE OF INSTITUTES

Can. 673 — The Apostolate of all religious consists first in their witness of a consecrated life which they are bound to foster by prayer and penance.

Can. 674 — Institutes which are wholly ordered to contemplation always retain a distinguished position in the mystical Body of Christ; for they offer an extraordinary sacrifice of praise to God, they illuminate the people of God with the richest fruits of their sanctity, they move it by their example, and extend it through their hidden apostolic fruitfulness. For this reason, however much the needs of the active apostolate demand it, members of these institutes cannot be summoned to aid in various pastoral ministries.

Can. 675 — §1. In institutes dedicated to works of the apostolate, apostolic action pertains to their very nature. Hence, the whole life of members is to be imbued with an apostolic spirit, indeed the whole apostolic action is to be informed by a religious spirit.

§2. Apostolic action is always to proceed from an intimate union with God, and it is to confirm and foster that union.

§3. Apostolic action, to be exercised in the name and by the mandate of the Church, is to be carried out in its communion.

Can. 676 — Lay institutes, whether of men or women, share in the pastoral office of the Church through spiritual and corporal works of mercy and offer the most diverse services to men and women; therefore they are to persevere faithfully in the grace of their vocation.

Can. 677 — §1. Superiors and members are faithfully to retain the mission and works proper to the institute; nevertheless they are to accommodate these prudently to the needs of times and places, including the use of new and appropriate means.

§2. Moreover, if they have associations of the Christian faithful related to them, institutes are to assist them with special care so that they are imbued with a genuine spirit of their family.

Can. 678 — §1. Religious are subject to the authority of bishops, whom they are obliged to follow with devoted humility and respect, in those matters which involve the care of souls, the public exercise of divine worship and other works of the apostolate.

§2. In exercising an external apostolate, religious are also subject to their own superiors and must remain faithful to the discipline of the institute, which obligation bishops themselves should not fail to insist upon in cases which warrant it.

§3. In organizing the works of the apostolate of religious, it is necessary that diocesan bishops and religious superiors proceed after consultation with each other.

Can. 679 — When a most serious reason demands it a diocesan bishop can prohibit a member of a religious institute from living in his diocese; if the major superior of that religious has been advised and neglects to act, the matter is to be referred to the Holy See immediately.

Can. 680 — Among the various institutes and also between them and the secular clergy, orderly cooperation as well as a coordination of all apostolic works and activities, under the direction of the diocesan bishop, with due regard for the character and purpose of individual institutes and the laws of the foundation, is to be promoted.

Can. 681 — §1. Works which are entrusted to religious by the diocesan bishop are subject to the authority and direction of this same bishop, with due regard for the right of religious superiors according to the norm of can. 678, §§2 and 3.

§2. In these cases a written agreement is to be drawn up between the diocesan bishop and the competent superior of the institute, which, among other things, expressly and accurately defines what pertains to the work to be carried out, the members to be devoted to this, and economic matters.

Can. 682 — §1. If there is a question of conferring an ecclesiastical office in the diocese upon a certain religious, the religious is appointed by the diocesan bishop, following presentation by or at least assent of the competent superior.

§2. A religious can be removed from the office entrusted to him or her either at the discretion of the authority who entrusted it, after having notified the religious superior, or at the discretion of the superior, having notified the authority; and neither requires the consent of the other.

Can. 683 — §1. At the time of the pastoral visitation and also in case of necessity the diocesan bishop, either in person or through someone else, can make a visitation of the churches of religious or of their oratories, which the Christian faithful habitually attend, schools and other works of religion or charity, whether temporal or spiritual, entrusted to religious; however he may not visit schools which are open only to students belonging to the institute.

§2. But if by chance he discovers abuses and has advised the religious superior in vain, he himself can provide for it on his own authority.

Chapter vi
SEPARATION OF MEMBERS FROM THE INSTITUTE

Art. 1
Transfer to Another Institute

Can. 684 — §1. A member in perpetual vows cannot transfer from one religious institute to another without the permission of the supreme moderator of each institute given with the consent of their respective councils.

§2. After completing a probationary period which is to last at least three years, the member can be admitted to perpetual profession in the new institute. However, if the member refuses to make this profession or is not admitted to making it by competent superiors, the member is to return to the former institute, unless an indult of secularization has been obtained.

§3. For a religious to transfer from an autonomous monastery to another of the same institute or federation or confederation, it is required and is sufficient to have the consent of the major superior of both monasteries and the chapter of the receiving monastery, with due regard for other requirements determined in proper law; a new profession is not required.

§4. Proper law is to determine the time and mode of probation which is to precede the profession of a member in the new institute.

§5. For one to transfer to a secular institute or a society of apostolic life or from them to a religious institute permission of the Holy See is required, and its mandates are to be observed.

Can. 685 — §1. Until the religious makes profession in the new institute, while the vows remain, the rights and obligations which the member had in the former institute are suspended; however, the religious is obligated to observe the proper law of the new institute from the beginning of the probationary period.

§2. By profession in the new institute the member is incorporated into it, while the preceding vows, rights and obligations cease.

Art. 2
Departure from the Institute

Can. 686 — §1. With the consent of the council the supreme moderator for a grave reason can grant an indult of exclaustration to a member professed of perpetual vows, but not for more than three years, and with the prior consent of the local ordinary where he must remain if this concerns a cleric. Extending the indult or granting it for more than three years is reserved to the Holy See or, if there is question of institutes of diocesan right, to the diocesan bishop.

§2. It belongs to the Apostolic See alone to grant an indult of exclaustration for nuns.

§3. If a supreme moderator with the consent of the council petitions, exclustration can be imposed by the Holy See on a member of an institute of pontifical right or by a diocesan bishop on a member of an institute of diocesan right for grave reasons, with equity and charity being observed.

Can. 687 — Exclaustrated members are free from obligations which are incompatible with their new condition of life and at the same time remain dependent on and subject to the care of their superiors and also the local ordinary, especially if the member is a cleric. The members may wear the habit of the institute unless it is determined otherwise in the indult. However, they lack active and passive voice.

Can. 688 — §1. Whoever wishes to leave an institute when the time of profession has expired can depart from it.

§2. During the time of temporary profession whoever asks to leave the institute for a grave reason can be granted an indult to leave by the supreme moderator in an institute of pontifical right with the consent of the council; in institutes of diocesan right and in monasteries mentioned in can. 615, the indult, in order to be valid, must be confirmed by the bishop of the house of assignment.

Can. 689 — §1. If just causes are present, when temporary profession has expired a member can be excluded from making a subsequent profession by the competent major superior after listening to the council.

§2. Even if it is contracted after profession, physical or psychic illness which in the judgment of experts renders the member mentioned in §1 unsuited to lead the life of the institute, constitutes a reason for not admitting such a person to a renewal of profession or to making perpetual profession, unless the infirmity had been incurred through the institute's negligence or through work performed in the institute.

§3. A religious, however, who becomes insane during temporary vows, even though unable to make a new profession, cannot be dismissed from the institute.

Can. 690 — §1. A religious who after completing the novitiate or after profession has left the institute legitimately, can be readmitted by the supreme moderator with the consent of the council without the burden of repeating the novitiate; it is up to the same moderator to determine a suitable probationary period before temporary profession and a time in such vows prior to perpetual profession according to the norm of cann. 655 and 657.

§2. With the consent of the council, the superior of an autonomous monastery enjoys this same faculty.

Can. 691 — §1. One who is professed in perpetual vows is not to seek an indult to leave the institute without very grave reasons weighed before the Lord; such a petition is to be presented to the supreme moderator of the institute, who is to transmit it to the competent authority with a personal opinion and that of the council.

§2. An indult of this kind in institutes of pontifical right is reserved to the Apostolic See; but in institutes of diocesan right the diocesan bishop of the house of assignment can also grant it.

Can. 692 — Unless it has been rejected by the member in the act of notification, an indult legitimately granted and made known to the member brings with it, by the law itself, a dispensation from vows and from all obligations arising from profession.

Can. 693 — If the member is a cleric, the indult is not granted before he finds a bishop who will incardinate him into a diocese or at least receive him experimentally. If he is received experimentally, he is incardinated into the diocese by the law itself after five years have passed, unless the bishop has refused him.

Art. 3
Dismissal of Members

Can. 694 — §1. A member is to be held to be *ipso facto* dismissed from the institute who:
  1° has notoriously abandoned the Catholic faith;
  2° has contracted marriage or has attempted it, even only civilly.
§2. In these instances the major superior with the council without any delay and after having collected proofs should issue a declaration of the fact so that the dismissal is established juridically.

Can. 695 — §1. A member must be dismissed for the offenses in cann. 1397, 1398 and 1395, unless in the delicts mentioned in can. 1395, §2, the superior judges that dismissal is not entirely necessary and that the correction of the member and restitution of justice and reparation of scandal can be sufficiently assured in some other way.
§2. In these cases the major superior, having collected proofs about the facts and imputability, is to make known the accusation and the proofs to the member who is about to be dismissed, giving the member the opportunity of self-defense. All the acts, signed by the major superior and a notary, along with the written and signed responses of the member, are to be transmitted to the supreme moderator.

Can. 696 — §1. A member can also be dismissed for other causes, provided that they are grave, external, imputable and juridically proven, such as: habitual neglect of the obligations of consecrated life; repeated violations of the sacred bonds; pertinacious disobedience to lawful prescriptions of superiors in a serious matter; grave scandal arising from the culpable behavior of the member; pertinacious upholding or spreading of doctrines condemned by the magisterium of the Church; public adherence to ideologies infected by materialism or atheism; unlawful absence mentioned in can. 665, §2 lasting six months; other causes of similar seriousness which may be determined by the proper law of the institute.

§2. Even causes of lesser seriousness determined in proper law suffice for the dismissal of a member in temporary vows.

Can. 697 — In the cases mentioned in can. 696, if the major superior, after having heard the council, believes the process of dismissal is to be begun:

1° the major superior is to collect or complete proofs;

2° the major superior is to warn the member in writing or before two witnesses with an explicit threat of subsequent dismissal unless the member reforms, the cause of the dismissal is to be clearly indicated and the member is to be given the full opportunity of self-defense; but if the warning is in vain the superior is to proceed to a second warning, after an intervening time of at least fifteen days;

3° if this warning also has been in vain and the major superior with the council believes that there is sufficient proof of incorrigibility and that the defenses of the member are insufficient, and fifteen days have elapsed since the last warning without any effect, the major superior is to transmit to the supreme moderator all acts, signed by the major superior and a notary, along with the signed response of the member.

Can. 698 — In all cases mentioned in cann. 695 and 696, the right of a member to communicate with and offer a defense directly to the supreme moderator always remains intact.

Can. 699 — §1. With the council, which must have at least four members for validity, the supreme moderator is to proceed collegially to the careful weighing of the proofs, arguments and defenses; if it has been so decided by a secret ballot, the supreme moderator is to issue the decree of dismissal, with the motives in law and in fact expressed at least in summary fashion for validity.

§2. In autonomous monasteries mentioned in can. 615 the decision of dismissal pertains to the diocesan bishop, to whom the superior is to submit the acts examined by the council.

Can. 700 — A decree of dismissal does not take effect unless it has been confirmed by the Holy See to whom the decree and all the acts are to be transmitted; if it is a question of an institute of diocesan right, the confirmation belongs to the bishop of the diocese where the house to which the religious is assigned is situated. The decree, for validity, must indicate the right which the dismissed religious enjoys to have recourse to competent authority within ten days from receiving the notification. The recourse has a suspensive effect.

Can. 701 — Vows, rights and obligations derived from profession cease *ipso facto* by legitimate dismissal. However, if the member is a cleric, he cannot exercise sacred orders until he finds a bishop who receives him after a suitable probationary period in the diocese according to can. 693 or at least allows him to exercise sacred orders.

Can. 702 — §1. Those who have legitimately left a religious institute or have been legitimately dismissed from one can request nothing from it for any work done in it.

§2. The institute however is to observe equity and evangelical charity toward the member who is separated from it.

Can. 703 — In the case of serious exterior scandal or very grave imminent harm to the institute a member can be immediately expelled from the religious house by the major superior, or, if there is a danger in delay, by the local superior with the consent of the council. If it is necessary the major superior should see that the process of dismissal is begun according to the norm of law or refer the matter to the Apostolic See.

Can. 704 — The report to be sent to the Apostolic See referred to in canon 592, §1 is to mention members separated from the institute in any way whatsoever.

CHAPTER VII
RELIGIOUS RAISED TO THE EPISCOPATE

Can. 705 — A religious raised to the episcopate remains a member of his own institute but is subject to the Roman Pontiff alone in virtue of the vow of obedience and is not bound by obligations which he himself prudently judges cannot be reconciled with his position.

Can. 706 — As regards the above-mentioned religious:

1° if through profession he has lost the ownership of goods, he has the use of goods which come to him as well as their revenues and administration; however the diocesan bishop and those mentioned in can. 381, §2 acquire the ownership for the particular church; all others, for the institute or the Holy See depending on whether the institute is capable of ownership or not;

2° if through profession he has not lost the ownership of goods, he regains the use, revenues and administration of the goods which he had; he fully acquires for himself those which come to him afterwards;

3° in either case, however, he must distribute goods coming to him according to the will of the donors when they do not come to him for personal reasons.

Can. 707 — §1. A retired religious bishop may choose a place to live for himself even outside the houses of his institute unless something else has been provided by the Apostolic See.

§2. If he has served a certain diocese, suitable and worthy sustenance is to be his according to can. 402, §2 unless his own institute wishes to provide that sustenance; otherwise the Apostolic See is to provide.

Chapter VIII
CONFERENCES OF MAJOR SUPERIORS

Can. 708 — Major superiors can usefully associate in conferences or councils so that joining forces they can work toward the achievement of the purpose of their individual institutes more fully, always with due regard for their autonomy, character and particular spirit, transact common business and foster suitable coordination and cooperation with conferences of bishops and also with individual bishops.

Can. 709 — Conferences of major superiors are to have their own statutes approved by the Holy See, by which alone they can be erected, even as a juridic person, and under whose supreme governance they remain.

Glossary

alienation—acts (such as selling, giving, leasing, etc.) that transfer or seriously burden the right of ownership of goods (c. 638)

apostolic constitution—formal, solemn document, often legislative, issued by the Holy See dealing with important matters of concern to the universal church

common life—(strict sense) dwelling together under a common roof, sharing lodging, board and daily life in a familial manner; (broad sense) membership in an institute that is a juridic person with a determined superior and definite rule

competent authority—designated person or group having the power to act validly according to law in a particular situation (i.e., diocesan bishop, major superior, general chapter, etc.)

consecrated life—term used in the new code to refer to the categories of religious institute (c. 607), secular institute (c. 710), hermits (c. 603) and the order of virgins (c. 604)

council—an advisory group of several members of the institute whose advice or consent must be sought by superiors in a prescribed manner in certain instances (c. 627)

decree (general)—a document issued by the competent authority which either enacts legal prescriptions or determines the methods to apply the law or urges observance of laws (cc. 29–31)

diocesan bishop—a bishop who is in charge of a diocese (c. 381) or a priest or bishop in charge of what is legally equivalent to a diocese (cc. 134.3, 381.2, 368) dismissal—precise legal procedure whose effect renders a person no longer a member of a religious institute (cc. 694–702)

dispensation from vows—legal consequence of no longer being bound by one's vows subsequent to an indult of departure (c. 692) or dismissal (c. 701).

exclaustration—living outside the institute while legally remaining a member of the institute but with mitigated rights and obligations; it may be requested by the member or imposed by competent authority (cc. 686–687)

exemption—removal of an institute from the direct authority of the local ordinary so that it is subject to the pope or to some other authority in internal matters (c. 591)

faculty—special grant of power to an individual (or group) so that one may act in a matter in which the action would otherwise be invalid (c. 132)

general chapter—a representative body authorized to elect the supreme moderator, deal with major business, and publish binding norms for an institute in addition to the power defined for it in the constitutions of the institute (c. 631)

house—technical term referring to a public juridic person established by the competent authority of the institute with the previous written consent of the diocesan bishop (cc. 609–616)

incorporation—becoming legally a member of a religious institute by profession of public vows (c. 654)

indult—a favor granted by the competent authority (such as, an "indult of departure" or and "indult of exclaustration")

instruction—binding documents issued by competent authorities within the limits of their power clarifying a law or elaborating on or determining the manner of implementation of a law (c. 34)

ius vigens—the law that is currently flourishing or actually in effect at the moment

Glossary

juridic person—a legal entity (formerly known as a "moral person" and *somewhat* comparable to a civil law corporation) that is the subject of rights (such as, the ability to conduct legal transactions like buying and selling) and which is independent from the persons or things comprising it (cc. 113–123). For example, a religious institute is by law a public juridic person (c. 634) which is distinct from the members or buildings of the institute.

law—an ordinance of reason formulated by one who has care for the common good and promulgated (Note: this is the definition used by but nowhere contained in the code.)

"leave of absence"—a phrase misused with respect to religious institutes to refer to the possibility of "lengthy absence from the house" that can be granted by the major superior under certain circumstances according to c. 665.1 but which does not alter the legal status of the member (as does exclaustration) in any way

local ordinary (also "ordinary of the place")—pope, diocesan bishops, and those equivalent to diocesan bishops legally, as well as those who have executive power which is attached by law to the office they hold (such as, episcopal vicars); the major superior of a clerical religious institute of pontifical right is an ordinary but not a "local ordinary" (c.134.1)

major superior—those who govern an entire institute or a province (or a part equivalent to a province) or a *sui iuris* house, as well as the legal vicars of these persons (c. 620)

motu proprio—a document issued on the initiative of the competent authority (as opposed to requested by another) and which is usually legislative in import

papal cloister—norms enacted by the Holy See for cloistered contemplative women which regulate various aspects of the lives of the nuns as well as conditions under which the nuns may exit from or others may have access to restricted areas of the monastery (c. 667) patrimony—personal property that legally belongs to an individual religious provided he or she has not completely renounced ownership of goods by the nature of profession in the religious institute (c. 668)

power of governance (also known as "jurisdiction")—that power in the Church by divine institution which is distinguished as legislative, executive and judicial and is governed by cc. 129–144

proper law—law enacted for a particular institute (in contrast to particular law which is enacted for certain territories or to universal law which is enacted for the entire Church)

province—a grouping of houses under the same superior (a provincial) established as a juridic person as a subdivision of the institute (c. 621)

religious—one who has made profession in a religious institute according to cc. 607, 654

rescript—a written reply to some request or question

SCRSI (also abbreviated as SCRIS)—the Sacred Congregation for Religious and Secular Institutes or department of the Roman Curia competent in matters concerning these institutes directly for pontifical institutes (established or approved by the Holy See) and directly in some but indirectly in other matters (such as approval of constitutions) for diocesan institutes (established by a diocesan bishop) (cc. 589, 593–595)

sui iuris—autonomous or "self-governing" with respect to government and discipline

supreme moderator—one who has power over an entire institute, its provinces, houses and members (c. 622)

transfer—change of a member's legal incorporation from one religious institute to another (cc. 684–685)

vow—free and deliberate promise made to God of a possible greater good; a vow is public (rather than private) or solemn (rather than simple) if recognized by the Church as such (cc. 1191–1192)

Index of Topics

Admission, 53
　see cc. 641–645
　re-admission, 54
Apostolate, 38, 60, 68, 71
　see cc. 673–683
　accommodation of, 71
　and legitimately established
　　house, 71
　cooperation in, 39
　restrictions of, 71
　written agreements, 39
Apostolic See, 49, 52
　see cc. 579, 582–584, 589, 592–
　　593, 595, 609, 616, 667, 686,
　　691, 703–704
Approbation of institutes, 37, 38, 39
　see cc. 579, 583, 587, 589
Authority
　see c. 608
　and obedience, 64
　as hierarchical, 67
　as service, 65
　canonical understanding, 64
　of God, 64
　of religious superiors, 39
　　see cc. 596, 617–619
　personal exercise of, 65

Canon law
　history of, 9
　　Carolingian Empire, 11
　　church orders, 10
　　civil legislation, 11

Corpus Iuris Canonici, 13
　Decretals, 12
　early collections, 10
　early reforms, 11
　Eastern legislation, 11
　first codification, 13
　first official collection, 13
　Middle Ages, 13
　Roman Empire, 10
　Trent, 13
Canonical approbation, 38
　see Approbation of institutes
Canons of the 1983 Code
　English translation, see Appendix
　　V
　format of, 44
　on consecrated life (573–606), 35
　on religious institutes (607–714),
　　35
Chaplains, 52
Charism, 40, 68–69
Chastity, 36
　see c. 599
Cloister, see contemplatives
　as privacy, 87
　current law regarding, 81
　see also c. 667
　for women,
　　and Council of Trent, 77
　　and development of active apos-
　　　tolates, 77
　　and French revolution, 77
　　and solemn vows, 76

159

Cloister (*continued*)
  as contemplative space, 88
  current canon regarding, 83
  current legislation, 81ff, 85ff
  extern sisters, 79
  former law regarding, 79ff
  former penalties for violation of, 79
  history of, 75ff
  material separation, 87
  medieval legislation on, 76
  papal, 83
  Pius XII and norms on, 80
  post-1917 code norms regarding, 80
  revision of post-1917 code norms, 83
  Venite seorsum, 83ff
  violation of, 79
Code of 1917, 14
  divisions of, 42–44
Code of 1983
  divisions of, 42–44
  evaluation of revision, 15
  of Justinian, 11
  principles for revision, 14
  revision, 15
Common life, 38, 57
  see c. 607
  in *Perfectae caritatis,* 59
Community, 61
  see common life
  see cc. 602, 608
Concordance of Discordant Canons, 12
  see Canon law-History
Confession, 50, 52
  see c. 630
Consecration
  personal, 36
Contemplative institutes, 38
  see cloister
Contemplatives, *see* cloister
  and apostolate, 68
  vocation of, 86ff
Corpus Iuris Canonici, see Canon law-History
Council
  see c. 627
  requirement for in religious institutes, 38
Curia (Roman), 49
Custom, 94

Decretals, *see* Canon law-History
Decretum, 12
  see Canon law-History
Diocesan Bishop, 70
  and apostolate, 70
  cooperation with superiors, 72
  in relation to monasteries, 82
Diocese, 39
Dismissal, 54
  see cc. 694–701
  procedure, 50, 54
  rejection of decree, 54

Elections, 52
  see cc. 625–626
Exclaustration, 54
  see cc. 686–687
  effects of, 54
  imposed, 54
Exemption, 48
  see c. 591

Fallacies regarding law, 94
Finance council, 53
Formation, 36, 49
  see cc. 659–661

General chapters, 38, 39, 67
  see cc. 631–632
  see also Appendix IV
Government, 70
Gratian, 12
  see also Canon law-History

Hermits, 52
  see c. 603
House, 38
  see cc. 608–616
  absence from, 47, 60
  legitimately established, 60, 71
  related to common life, 60
  religious, 60
Houses
  and apostolate, 71
  and superiors, 60, 61

Index

Institutes, types of
  clerical, 52
    see also c. 588
  diocesan, *see* cc. 579, 595
  lay, 52
    see also c. 588
Interim legislation, 46ff
  see also Appendix III
  Ad instituenda, 49
  Christus Dominus, 48
  Cum admotae, 47
  Cum superiores, 49
  Deserunt praebendo, 50
  Dum canonicarum, 50
  Ecclesiae sanctae, 48
  Lumen gentium, 44, 47
  Pastorale munus, 47
  Perfectae caritatis, 45, 48
  Processus iudicialis, 50
  Regimini ecclesiae, 49
  Religionum laicalium, 48
  Renovationis causam, 49
  Venite seorsum, 83
Interpretation, 60, 93
Ius vigens, 45, 50, 51

John XXIII, 14
Juridic person, 37
  public, 53
  related to common life, 58
Jurisdiction, 68, 70
Justice of God, 3
Justification, 3

Law
  nomos, 1
  and innovation, 21
  and presumptions, 20
  and prophecy, 21
  and sacraments, 19, 23
  and the Spirit, 2, 7
  and theology, 19
  as burden, 7
  as communication, 25
  as service, 19
  biblical notion of, 1, 97
  canon, *see* Canon Law
  definition of, 20
  evolution of, 9
  functions of, 22
  in Romans and Galatians, 2
  internal, 2
  interpretation of, 60, 93
  levels of documentation for, 26, 94
  limitations of, 24
  misuse of, 6, 28, 30
  Mosaic, 1, 2, 3
  necessity of, 5
  of Christ, 1, 2
  proper, 34
  purpose of, 19
  response to, 91ff
  role of, 19
  universal, 34
Legislative power, 67
  see also Appendix IV
Limitations of law, 24
  contextual, 27
  documentation, 26
  human misuse, 28
  literary forms, 25
  presumptions, 24
Local ordinary, 70
  see Diocesan Bishop

Major superiors
  see c. 620
  conferences of
    see Perfectae caritatis in Appendix III
  of monasteries, 81ff
Misuse of law, 30
Monastery
  see cc. 609, 614–616, 667
  and vigilance of diocesan bishop, 82
  of nuns, 82
    founding, 82
    suppression, 82
  self-governing, 82
Monks, 82
  see c. 613

Novitiate, 49, 53
  see cc. 646–653
  see also Renovationis causam and Appendix III
  transfer of house, 49

Obedience, 36, 61
  see c. 601
  and authority, 61, 64
  vow of, 64, 65
Order of virgins, 52
  see c. 604

Pachomius, 57
Particular church, 39
Patrimony
  see c. 668
  renunciation of, 47
Poverty, 36
  vow of, see c. 600
Power, see jurisdiction
  of governance, 70
Presumptions, 33
  in law, 20
Procedures in law, 23
Profession
  see cc. 654–658
  see also Appendix IV
  first, 53
  nonadmission to renewal of or to perpetual, 54
Promises
  in *Renovationis causam*, 49, 53
  see cc. 607, 654
  see also Appendix III and Appendix IV
Proper law, 34, 38
Property
  ownership by juridic person, 37
Public vows, 36
  see cc. 607, 654

Religious
  and labor unions, 71
  and obligations of clerics, 54
  apostolate of, 71
  in 1917 code, 44ff
  in 1983 code, 44ff
  in public office, 71
  nuns, 78
  obligations of, 53
  regulars, 78
  sisters, 78
Religious law
  evolution of, 16
Religious life
  as following of Christ, 34, 35, 36, 98

  as personal consecration, 36
  essentials of, 33, 39
  renewal of, 46
Roman law, 44

Sacred Congregation for Religious & Secular Institutes (SCRSI), 49
Secular institutes, 45
Superior, 39
  see cc. 617–619
  pope as highest, 38, 65
Superiors
  cooperation of with bishops, 70
  in houses, 61, 70
  limits of authority, 70
  personal authority, 38
  responsibilities of, 69–70
  Roman Pontiff as, 38, 70

Temporal goods, 52
  see cc. 634–640
Transfer, 54
  see cc. 684–685
Trent, 13
  see Canon Law-History

Universal law, 34, 40

Vatican Council I, 13
Vatican Council II, 14, 33, 44, 45, 46, 71, 93
  and contemplative life, 83
Vow
  of chastity, 36
    see c. 599
  of obedience, 36
    see c. 601
  of poverty, 36
    see c. 600
  public, 53
    see Appendix IV
  simple, 53, 78
  solemn, 53, 78
Vows, 36
  obligations resulting from, 71
  see cc. 662–672

Will, 50
  see c. 668

Index of Canons

Canons of 1983 Code	Page
cc. 113–123,	37
c. 120,	37
c. 129,	70
cc. 129–144,	70
c. 134,	70
cc. 164–179,	52
c. 285,	71
c. 287,	71
c. 381,	70
c. 573,	35, 48
cc. 573–575,	48
cc. 573–606,	34, 51
c. 576,	36–37, 69, 72
cc. 576–578,	48
c. 577,	69
c. 578,	48, 69
c. 579,	37
c. 581,	51
c. 584,	37
c. 586,	37
c. 587,	37, 48, 69
c. 588,	52, 69
c. 589,	70
c. 590,	38, 65
cc. 590–591,	48
c. 591,	70
c. 595,	37, 52
c. 596,	38
c. 598,	35, 67
c. 599,	35, 36
cc. 599–602,	48
c. 600,	35, 36

c. 601,	35, 36, 65
c. 602,	59
c. 604,	52
c. 607,	36, 38, 48, 49, 53, 59
c. 608,	38, 48, 59, 61, 66
c. 609,	82
cc. 609ff,	60
c. 611,	71
c. 613,	82
c. 615,	82
c. 616,	60, 83
c. 617,	36, 38
c. 618,	65
c. 619,	35, 36, 66
c. 622,	36
c. 623,	67
c. 624,	67
c. 625,	36, 52, 82
c. 626,	38, 67
c. 627,	38, 67
c. 628,	82
c. 629,	60, 61, 66
c. 630,	36, 48, 50, 52, 87
c. 631,	38, 67
cc. 631–633,	67
c. 634,	37, 60
cc. 634–640,	52
c. 637,	82
c. 638,	82
c. 640,	48
c. 641,	53
c. 642,	36, 53
c. 643,	53
c. 646,	49
cc. 647–649,	53
c. 652,	36, 48
c. 654,	36, 49, 53, 67
c. 655,	49
c. 656,	53
c. 657,	49
c. 658,	53
c. 659,	48
c. 661,	35, 48
c. 662,	35, 48
cc. 662–664,	54
c. 663,	35, 54
c. 665,	38, 48, 59
c. 666,	85
c. 667,	36, 47, 80–81, 83, 87
c. 668,	47, 50

Index

c. 669,	48
c. 670,	36
c. 671,	71
c. 672,	54, 71
c. 673,	38, 48, 68, 72
c. 674,	38, 48, 68
c. 675,	38, 48, 68
cc. 675–677,	72
c. 677,	48, 72
c. 678,	39, 48, 71
cc. 678–679,	70
c. 679,	47, 70
c. 680,	39
c. 681,	39, 70
cc. 682–683,	70
c. 683,	39
c. 684,	47, 54
c. 686,	54
c. 687,	54
c. 688,	47, 49
c. 689,	50, 54
c. 690,	49, 54
c. 697,	50
cc. 697–700,	50, 54
c. 699,	82
c. 702,	50
cc. 708–709,	48
c. 1191,	36
c. 1192,	36, 53

610069